PEN
THE MAN W...

Dalip Singh Rana, aka The Great Khali, is a former WWE World Heavyweight Champion. As the first major Indian wrestler in the WWE arena, he became a sensation with a huge international fan following. Described as one of the most powerful professional wrestlers in history, he lives with his wife and daughter in Jalandhar, and juggles his time between movies, TV shows and running a training academy for professional wrestling.

Vinit K. Bansal is a banker by profession and a writer by passion. Having edited and compiled the hugely successful Uff Ye Emotions series, he has also authored books like *I Am Heartless* and *Soulmates,* both of which became bestsellers.

THE MAN WHO BECAME KHALI

DALIP SINGH RANA
WITH
VINIT K. BANSAL

PENGUIN BOOKS

PENGUIN BOOKS

USA | Canada | UK | Ireland | Australia
New Zealand | India | South Africa | China

Penguin Books is part of the Penguin Random House group of companies whose addresses can be found at global.penguinrandomhouse.com

Published by Penguin Random House India Pvt. Ltd
7th Floor, Infinity Tower C, DLF Cyber City,
Gurgaon 122 002, Haryana, India

First published in Penguin Books by Penguin Random House India 2017

Copyright © Dalip Singh Rana 2017

All rights reserved

10 9 8 7 6 5 4 3 2 1

The views and opinions expressed in this book are the authors' own and the facts are as reported by them which have been verified to the extent possible, and the publishers are not in any way liable for the same.

ISBN 9780143426233

For sale in the Indian Subcontinent only

Typeset in Adobe Garamond Pro by Manipal Digital Systems, Manipal
Printed at Thomson Press India Ltd, New Delhi

This book is sold subject to the condition that it shall not, by way of trade or otherwise, be lent, resold, hired out, or otherwise circulated without the publisher's prior consent in any form of binding or cover other than that in which it is published and without a similar condition including this condition being imposed on the subsequent purchaser.

www.penguin.co.in

To the love of my life—my wife, Harpinder—and my fans all around the world

Contents

Prologue	ix
1. My Childhood Days	1
2. My First Earning—Rs 5	6
3. The Story of the Underwear	11
4. A Lesson for Life	16
5. An Escape	22
6. Such a Mess	28
7. One Desperate Attempt	37
8. My First 'Real' Job	44
9. Fights outside the Ring	54
10. The Turning Point of My Life	63
11. My Failures in Sports	79
12. Warm Up	88
13. And the Real Fight Starts	96
14. Making of the Real Beast	104
15. The First Step	112
16. The Love of My Life	117

17. An Unseen World	127
18. Opening My Own Gym	132
19. A Difficult Coach	136
20. The Launch—A Surprise for the World	142
21. The WWE Championship	148
22. A Visit to My Homeland—India	151
23. The Kiss Cam	156
24. When Big Show Cried	160
25. A Reality Show	164
26. The Most Precious Gifts of My Life	167
27. CWE Academy—From Aspirations to Reality	173

Acknowledgements   177

Prologue

January 2014

It was a cold night, yet there was a feeling of warmth in my heart. I was happy to be back in India, to my homeland—Jalandhar—the city of peace. Being here always gives me an inexplicable feeling of pleasure as it is this city that transformed Dalip Singh Rana, an unknown constable, to The Great Khali, a World Wrestling Entertainment (WWE) champion.

This remarkable life would not have existed but for this city, its people and the God above. Being here takes me back to my past—bringing back memories of those dreary days of oblivion. Sometimes in life, there are moments when all we do is sit in silence and try to introspect. I was in such an emotional state that night. Who was I? Who knew me when I first came to this place? These questions kindled thoughts within me—about me, about my past life, about the time when I was nothing and about those moments when thousands of people screamed and cheered for me in the ring. It was an unforeseen journey and seems like a dream now. A dream, which was inconceivable during the years of my youth but which was part of my reality now. I was overwhelmed with emotion. Tears welled up in my eyes. These were the tears of happiness and contentment for something I had achieved only because of my admirers and because of God.

An incident from the previous day when I was in New Delhi crossed my mind.

I was driving my car and was stuck at a traffic light near the Raj Ghat area. In a few minutes, I saw some people call out my name in astonishment and, within no time, my car was surrounded by hundreds of people and the number increased with every passing second. The entire road was jammed in no time. People were cheering, tapping on my car, trying to shake hands with me and clicking pictures with their phones. Within a few minutes, the situation changed from bad to worse. I suddenly lost track of the number of people around me. There must have been more than a thousand. I was happy to see their love and affection for me. If I was in a public event or a professional fight, this would have been a normal thing, but this crowd was uncontrollable and it made me a little worried. I heard the Police Control Room (PCR) vans coming towards the crowd and forcing them to move away from the road. But it seemed ineffective. The policemen's crowd-control measures seemed to fail before the euphoria of the crowd. The swelling mass of people shouted my name over and over again, urging me to step out of my car. As this could have led to grave consequences, I decided against it.

I felt moved by the love of my fans, and to respect their love, I waved my hand at them. Thousands of people cheered in jubilation in front of me. I felt honoured. I felt blessed.

This was something I could never expect in the US. Here in India, people express their emotions more openly. I felt blissful. Later, it was the Delhi chief ministerial candidate's intervention that helped me get through the situation.

In the aura of these thoughts, I searched for my name on the Internet. Some might think that it was my ego that made me do it but I think it was simply because I wanted to see how my life was being projected on the Net. There were numerous news articles and blogs on me. While some of them praised me, others criticized. Some content was true but most of it was just bogus news. Gossip about my personal life, professional life, my diet and my body weight hung shamelessly on the Internet walls. The incorrect information made me restless. At that time, there were two things I could do. I could either take out my anger against the websites that displayed incorrect information, which in turn would lead to more malicious gossip, or I could ignore them, like many others did.

The next day, when I was sitting with one of my friends, I told him about the bogus news articles I had encountered the previous night. I also told him about my musings. It was a long talk and during our conversation, he suggested something I had never thought of. He gave me the idea to pen down my feelings in the form of a biography. It sounded strange to me. I'm not a man of words; I'm a man of action. I don't write books!

However, as the days passed by, I felt that, maybe, I should think about it seriously. This would be a story that I had never told anybody. My friends, family, media, my fans, well-wishers and even my wife—all know fractional parts of my life but not the entire story. My life, which to them seemed like a fairy tale, was not all plain sailing. So, finally, I took the decision to start a new journey—on paper.

And this is how I embarked on the journey of *The Man Who Became Khali* . . .

1

My Childhood Days

August 1972

It was that time of the year when the monsoon in India was at its peak and the weather was pleasantly cool. A time when the blazing heat of summer had given way to joyous drops of relief, and winter was still a long way ahead. The beauty of the valley was blissfully enriched because of the rains and the Himalayas were covered in an alpine flora cover.

Surrounded by this spectacular environment was a small village, Dhirana, which was home to not more than fifteen families. Located in the Sirmour district of Himachal Pradesh, it is among those thousands of Indian villages that lie out of the spotlight.

Within that small flock was one family I called mine. Ours was a family which, like many others, spent all its days striving to earn its daily bread and butter. Our single-minded focus on work made us oblivious to even the beauty of the valley surrounding us.

When I was born—I was the third child—my family was happy to know that there would now be a new earning hand. More children meant there were more labouring hands, which ultimately meant more inflow of money. Like all other families, my family too had a similar motive. I was thus born with a burden—the burden to support my family, to give them a better life and to improve our poverty-stricken condition as much as I could.

As I grew up, I slowly began to realize how each and every one was overloaded with work. My parents, my brothers and sisters had their own set of work. We were six by now—three brothers, a sister and my parents. From the first light of dawn till the end of the day, they were involved in doing something or the other. Perhaps they had a mission and wanted to gain something. But I was too young to understand the reason why everyone was so busy. Many a time, I was left alone in the house as the other members of the family were busy with work.

My father, Jwalaram, who was a farmer, used to work in our small farm of two acres, which was the family's only possession apart from two cows and two bullocks. Farming in the hilly areas is a tough job and is entirely dependent on the monsoon. Most of the time, the farm yield was just sufficient enough to feed the family and only a small amount was left for sale. My mother, Tundi Devi, was always busy taking care of the cattle and other household activities. Sometimes, she also helped my father in the fields. I loved to see my mother milking the cows. I also enjoyed watching and talking to the cows and bullocks when she took them for grazing.

The village didn't have any medical or transportation facilities. But luckily, there was a government primary school.

Though the financial condition of the family did not permit it, our parents were concerned about our education. I was thus sent to school.

The school was in no way similar to the modern schools that we see in cities today. It just had one small room. I don't have many memories of my school. There are only a few blurred and vague remembrances of a number of banyan trees under which classes were held and where we all had to sit on mats.

As a child, the letters of the alphabets seemed like unsolved puzzles to me. I could never understand why we had to draw a straight line moving downwards along with a small half-closed circle on one and an open circle on the other side for the letter 'क'. It took me a couple of months to learn the very first letter of the Hindi alphabet. This game of alphabets didn't appeal to me and most of the time it was tough for me to understand it. I can recollect an incident of my school life which is related to my inability to write the Hindi alphabets properly.

One day in class, our teacher was trying to make us learn the alphabet 'ख'. He tried to explain to me numerous times but I was making the same mistake over and over again. Then, the teacher told all the students to look at the board and write the alphabet in their notebooks. I couldn't understand what was being taught to me and tried to peep into the notebook of the student who was sitting ahead of me. Just at that moment, the teacher, who we used to address as 'Master ji', caught me in the act. I got slapped; not once, not twice, but three times. I had no idea how to react at that time. I was shocked for a moment. I stood in front of him and looked at his face, waiting for his next reaction. The teacher took it as a gesture of impudence. As punishment, I was made to squat on the floor holding my ears in front of the entire class. It was so humiliating that I have not forgotten it till date.

However, schooling didn't last very long for me. When I was in Class II, my family went through a severe financial crisis and there wasn't any money in the house, let alone to pay for school. My parents were worried about fulfilling our basic needs. I was somehow able to complete Class I, albeit with a lot of constraints, but it was tough for our family to pay the school fees for all the children. Our annual school fee was Rs 2.50 (it is really nothing in today's times) and even that was tough for my parents to pay.

By now, there were seven members in the family. Arranging even a meagre meal twice a day for all was not easy. Somehow, my parents continued to pay the fees for the education of all children. But for me, school wasn't a long-term goal and the turn of events was such that I couldn't continue.

It was the summer of 1979; the monsoon was awaited and there wasn't any money left for the fees since the crops had dried out. Almost a month had passed since I moved to Class II and the principal was accosting me on a daily basis for not paying the school fees. Then one day, my class teacher abused me in front of the entire class. The other students sneered at me and made fun of me. I didn't know how to react but that day I felt so bad that I left my class in between and rushed home. My father had gone out for some work and my mother was preparing food for us. I interrupted her and asked for the money. She tried to explain to me about the monetary problems our family was going through. She assured me that my father was trying to arrange the money for the fees and as soon as he was able to arrange it, it would be paid.

But I stuck to my decision and didn't go back to school that day. In the evening, a similar explanation was given to me by my father. I felt helpless. I didn't want to face a similar situation again, so when the next day, my mother woke me up and told me to get ready for school, I refused. I said that I would not go to school unless my fees were paid. My mother was unhappy with my reluctance and tried to persuade me many times, but I was adamant. My father said that he would talk to the principal but that didn't pacify me either and that was how school life ended for me.

My schooling ended forever and so did my education. My mind was inclined to work—to work for my family and to support my parents. I didn't want my younger brothers to face the same plight I had gone through. I wanted to work, earn and help to add to the income. I didn't like it when my mother didn't eat the last meal of the day because there was nothing left for her to eat after feeding me, my siblings and my father. The pain of poverty reached its highest level. It now required us to have resilience and to rebuild the course of our lives. This was how the next chapter of my life began. It was a beginning fraught with grief and sacrifice—one which was tough for the small shoulders of an eight-year-old child to bear.

Often, I observe people talk about their school and college life. As you know by now, for me, school didn't exist and neither did college. But even in the worst of times, I've believed in God and His powers. I know that even during those times, He was looking after me. So, if you are going through the worst phase of your life, remember that He is there to look after you.

2

My First Earning—Rs 5

June 1979

For several days, I stayed at home. Initially, I helped my mother in her household chores. I also liked to look after the cattle. I woke up early in the morning, took the cattle for grazing along the hills and also helped in milking the cows. When I prepared the husk for the cattle, it used to get stuck all over my body. My mother then helped me tidy up. After my bath, I would bathe the cattle and in the evening, I again took them for grazing. This routine continued for around three months. By now, the monsoon had arrived and the work at the farm was increasing. Hence, I changed my routine and started taking an interest in working at the farm. The processes of plantation intrigued me and I began to help my father in the farm.

One day, when I was with my father, the *mat* (account-keeper) came to him and informed him about a plantation job available in the village. He said that every worker would be paid a sum of Rs 5 per day.

As soon as I heard that, my eyes gleamed with excitement. For me, a sum of Rs 5 per day was a huge amount. It struck me that not long ago, we didn't even have Rs 2.50 for my school fees. Compared to that, Rs 5 seemed like a jackpot! I was motivated to work hard for it.

I was lost in excitement. Earning this money would help me pay the fees of two of my siblings. I felt as if I had landed an incredible opportunity. I wanted to do the job anyhow and informed the mat about my intentions. He looked at me with scorn and left the place. His reaction was natural as I was only eight years old at that time and the task demanded power and stamina. No eight-year-old was fit for the job.

But my mind would not take no for an answer. I needed the job and was ready to work hard for it. However, I was an eight-year-old at the end of the day and had to ask my father for help. Initially, he was reluctant and refused to listen, but later, my determination to help with the family's situation made him talk to the mat.

The very next day, I was in front of the mat once again. My father tried to convince him about my abilities. I was disappointed by his earlier refusal to let me work for him and did not want to be subjected to it again. He initially hesitated but when I reassured him of my dedication, he agreed and explained how to go about the work.

The work was with the forest department for its new campaign to plant some trees in the village. I had to work at the plant nursery, which was situated some 4 kilometres down the hill. I had to collect the plants, carry them on my back, travel uphill to the village for another 4 kilometres and plant them. Once all the trees were planted, I had to go back again and get more seedlings.

It was the day before I was to start work. The excitement about my new job didn't let me sleep. The next day I woke up before sunrise. Once awake, I saw that it was raining outside. In the hills, when there is heavy rainfall, it becomes difficult to walk down the hill. The soil becomes wet and there are high chances of losing balance, slipping on the mud and hurting oneself badly. Hence, we were often advised to not go down the hills during heavy rains. That day too, because of the harsh weather, I was told by my parents to not go out. But nothing would deter me. I felt as if this job was the biggest milestone I had crossed in my life and not even the heaviest rains could stop me.

I didn't listen to my parents and rushed out of my house. Since I had been told to reach the place by 8 a.m., I picked up my pace. The way to the nursery in the heavy downpour wasn't easy at all. I slipped a few times and the constant rains made it more and more difficult. But I didn't look back and continued walking.

When I reached the nursery, to my utter shock and confusion, I couldn't see a single soul there. There was absolutely no one around! I was in despair. The sudden happiness and excitement of reaching the nursery, working and earning was shattered. I roamed about and found a guard sitting there. When I inquired, he replied that due to the heavy rains no one had shown up yet. Seeing my dejected face, he suggested that I could wait if I wanted for them to arrive.

I decided to wait. By now, the rain had slowed down. It was merely a drizzle and yet no one came. The guard told me to come back the next day. I left the place completely dejected. I didn't sleep a wink that night. It was a dark and foreboding night. The moon was nowhere to be seen as if it was hiding behind a curtain of clouds. Just like the moon, I felt lost in desolation, trying to hide my feelings and my tears in a ragged blanket. I had been looking forward to my first earning but the day ended with no money in my hands. The rains had completely stopped by then and the sky was pitch-dark and still. I kept on tossing and turning throughout the night, waiting for sleep.

In the morning, I woke up with the same enthusiasm. The gloom of the previous night seemed like a forgotten thing. I got ready and rushed to the nursery. Fortunately, the work was in progress and the presence of the mat was a sign of relief for me. After talking to him, I picked up a sack full of seedlings and a spade. The mat instructed me to complete at least two rounds in the day, so I carried the sack of plants on my shoulder and went up the hill with great enthusiasm. At that time, I felt as if the sack of plants was no ordinary sack; it was a magic box which would gift me my first earning. I kept on walking briskly for the next two hours, planted the seedlings at the designated place and walked down to the nursery to collect more seedlings. The same routine continued for the entire day. I was so involved in the work that I even skipped lunch. Food was the last thing on my mind.

By evening, I realized that I had actually enjoyed the work and had developed an interest in planting the seedlings. When I went to the nursery, the mat was happy as I had completed three rounds of planting. He took out a small bag from his pocket and took out a note with five written on it and gave it to me.

That moment is still fresh in my mind, as if it was only yesterday. It was an inexplicable feeling, something that till date counts as one of my happiest memories.

My first earning! I was on cloud nine.

When I reached home, my mother was still in the kitchen waiting for me. I looked around for my father and spotted him lying on a *khaat,* a string bed, in the courtyard. I gave him the money. He stared at me for a few minutes. I saw tears welling up in his eyes but at that time I was too young to understand his emotions. He slowly patted my back and told me to give the money to my mother.

Perhaps, this was the moment when I stopped being a child. In just a day, I had shed the cloak of childhood and became an earning member of my family.

3

The Story of the Underwear

Due to my huge size, the only work I could do was manual labour. At this age, I was much taller and heavier in comparison to the children of my age. I was only eight years old, but I was as tall as five feet. I was a kid but looked like a grown-up. At an age when a child wishes to play with friends, I was always on the lookout for an opportunity where I would get the chance to earn some money. I removed huge pebbles, picked up sacks and worked throughout the day. I had no bedtime stories to listen to like the other children of my age. None of the people who worked with me was of my age, or even close. I wished I could do something better but my limitations didn't allow me to do so. Sometimes, I felt like crying. I felt pain in my heart, I felt lonely. I felt as if there was no one around me to care for me, but I was helpless. I had to work and earn.

Whenever I got to know about a job that required manual labour, I seized the opportunity.

However, my enthusiasm came with numerous challenges. I didn't bother about the difficulty level or my comfort. All that mattered was money. One such opportunity was brought by a distant relative, who happened to visit my home one day.

His name was Gyar Singh and I used to call him *tau ji*, which means an elder paternal uncle. Tau ji had good contacts with people in the contracting business. He informed us about an employment opportunity that would get me a sum of Rs 7 per day, but the only problem was that the work was outside the village. My job would be to collect *rohdi* (soft pebbles) from the banks of the mountain river and carry them to the nearby market. These pebbles were used as construction material in the hilly areas. Even though it was a challenging job, Rs 7 per day was too lucrative an offer for me to decline. I immediately agreed to do the job and along with tau ji and some other villagers, left for work.

It was only when the work commenced that I realized the difficulties and adversities were far bigger than I had imagined. I was the youngest person working there; all the others were at least twice my age. But I was taller and heavier than most of the workers in the vicinity and that helped me to do the strenuous work. Most of them had been doing this for a long time. Carrying the pebbles from the riverside was a task which involved a lot of risk. Getting to the *khad* (riverbed), which had a gravel path, was a big challenge. Slippery moss covered the banks of the river and the steepness of the khad increased the risk of losing one's balance. One needed to take utmost care to ensure that one did not fall. Sometimes, while collecting stones, we did fall and get hurt. Even though others fell too, I was particularly made fun of as I was the youngest.

We walked to the riverbed risking our lives. The summer season added to our woes as the pebbles heated up quickly, making it painful to walk over them. I couldn't afford to buy myself a pair of shoes and thus, I had to tread over the pebbles barefoot. Sometimes, when I was too scared of falling, I caught hold of my fellow mates' hand. This invited more jibes from the others. After collecting the pebbles in a sack, we had to carry them on our shoulders uphill. This again involved huge risks. Moving uphill with the weight on my shoulders on a gravel path further increased the chances of slipping. We had to walk for 7–8 kilometres to reach the market. Sometimes, midway, I used to get tired and sit on the roadside. The fellow workers would then mock me by saying, '*Itna bada shareer hai aur itna bhi nahi utha sakta? Tujhse na ho payega* (What's the use of having such a big body if you can't carry this much weight? You will never be able to do this task).'

They mocked me by repeating this statement over and over again. Apart from this, they conversed only among themselves. I had nobody to talk to. I was a loner. Sometimes, I would cry since there was no other way out. I felt ashamed because of my height. Many a time, I cursed myself for having been born with this kind of a physique. Why was I not like the others? Why was I so tall? A large number of such questions continued to haunt me all the time. I felt disheartened.

There was an embarrassing incident which, now when I look back, seems funny, too. The heat of the summer was too much to bear, therefore, all I used to wear was a *kaccha* (underwear tied at the waist with a string) and a kurta. Poverty did not give me the luxury of owning more than a single kaccha. One day, as I was working on the site, the string of the underwear suddenly tore and the kaccha slipped off! Since the kaccha was the only piece of cloth covering my lower body, I was stuck in the most awkward situation and had no idea what to do. Needless to say, I was once again the subject of mockery for the other fellow workers. I felt both embarrassed and helpless at the same time. Finally, I survived the day by clutching the string with one hand and carrying the load with the other. You can only imagine how it must have looked! In the evening, I got it repaired for 50 paisa. During those times, even 50 paisa was a huge amount of money.

Amidst tears and fears, I somehow managed to complete my job, but decided to leave as it was both physically and mentally exhausting. At the end of the month, a huge sum of Rs 210 was given to me and that seemed to make up for all the pain I had gone through.

After that, I continued to do small, odd jobs in the village. Sometimes, I got employment opportunities in the nearby villages as well. I would work in the morning and come back home in the evening. The wages weren't sufficient, but it was money at the end of the day.

I didn't want to miss a single opportunity to work as I wanted to earn money for my family. I couldn't afford to rest and sit at home for even a single day. The only thought that occupied my mind was the need to earn money and to make sure that all my brothers and sisters attend school and lead a decent and respectable life.

Besides my huge physique, my height also made me a laughing stock in the village. My face appeared to be lengthier in comparison to the other children of my age. My body seemed to be heavier than everyone around me. Why was I so tall? This was the most frequent question hurled at me like an insult by every person who met me. I stood apart from the crowd. Whenever someone made fun of me, I asked God in despair why he made me like this. My physique was like a curse and even my parents did not know how I had inherited it. Though, sometimes, I used to think that it was because of my physique that I was able to work and help my family. So, somewhere in my mind, I felt that it was a blessing in disguise.

4

A Lesson for Life

For an entire year, my life continued in a similar fashion. There wasn't anything out of the ordinary to do. I continued to do the usual odd jobs within the village and on rare occasions, outside it. Most of the jobs lasted a week or two; I didn't have a permanent job. Hence, each and every day used to be a fight with destiny. Sometimes, when I got a job, I felt victorious while at other times when I didn't, I felt like a loser. Amidst all these ups and downs, my childhood was lost. I kept oscillating between moments of happiness and dejection. It seemed as if there wasn't any job in this world that was meant for me.

Gradually, I came to terms with my predicaments and became content with my life. Even though my schooling had come to an end and I no longer had anyone to play with, it didn't bother me. I didn't think about the life I was missing as a child. Instead, my odd jobs kept me busy and I found tranquillity in those few coins I earned with my hard work. For me, earning money was what life was about.

Then in the year 1981, I came to know about a contractor who was looking for workers for a road construction project outside the village for a duration of three months. I was told that I would be offered a sum of Rs 15 per day. This leap from a meagre sum of Rs 7–8 to Rs 15 was huge! There was no way I could afford to lose out on this opportunity even though it involved leaving my house for the first time in my life and moving to a place I had never been to before. As the offer was irresistible, I didn't give it a second thought and accepted the work at once.

I left for the job the very next day. The work was in a village in Shimla. I was extremely excited. But once I reached there, I realized that everything that glitters is not gold. There were a large number of labourers and it was unlike the kind of work I was used to in my village. If the work I did there could be defined as hard work, then this changed the meaning of hard work. The workers were being exploited for money and I found it unbearable. We had to remove small and big rocks from the site so that a road could easily be built there. The worst part was that we didn't have any freedom. We had to live our life according to the orders given by the employers. They didn't care if we were tired or ill. For them, we were machines that could be run at any point of time.

Those three months constituted the most painful period for me. I worked from dawn till dusk. The food that was provided to us was so meagre that the other labourers and I often stayed on an empty stomach. There was no freedom and no respite. We were not allowed to move outside the site of construction and were subjected to the abuse of the contractor whenever we did something wrong. Even if anyone wasn't well, he or she would not be allowed to rest for even a single day. This was the first time when I saw humans working under the absolute control of another human. Slavery was the right term for what was happening.

During the plantation work back in the village, I thought I was the youngest person working as a labourer, but here, even children less than half my age were employed. Entire families were involved in the process of construction. The living conditions were pathetic and we were devoid of the basic facilities of life, such as adequate food, clothing and shelter. Subconsciously, I forgot how to smile and it seemed to me that the sole purpose of my life was work and more work. At night, I fell asleep as soon as I lay down, having completely exhausted both my mind and body. The room where I slept was made out of bamboo sticks, and more than a dozen people slept there on the floor.

The days spent there made me realize and appreciate the importance of home for the very first time. I understood the importance of being with one's family. No one was there to care for me. No one was there to ask whether I had eaten my food. No one scolded me for being dirty and unkempt. At home, I was never alone but there, I felt lonely and missed companionship. Home provided warmth and a feeling of completeness. Even amongst hundreds of people, there wasn't a single soul I could talk to or share my feelings with. I wasn't the only one going through this feeling of desolation. Everyone around me had the same story. However, many had their families with them and they could talk to each other in the evening. Twice during that time, I even thought of running back home. But then, I thought about the money—the coins and notes that made up a sum of Rs 15. That stopped me and I worked like a slave for three months.

After working so hard, it was time to rejoice. The day had come when I would be paid! I was excited that I would finally be getting what I was there for. When the project was completed, I was called for the payment. The contractor told me that due to the successful completion of the work within the given time, I would be given an additional payment of Rs 10 as a reward. My happiness on receiving the additional payment was phenomenal and all the anger I felt for the contractor seemed to vanish.

There were twenty-three notes, each of Rs 20. I tried to count them. I could not. I tried one more time and still could not! I had no idea how much they were but they seemed a lot. I didn't know what to do at that point of time. I kept on looking at the notes. I wanted to know how much the amount was. The guilt of not having completed my education struck me hard at that point.

I kept standing there for half an hour in a state of mixed emotions. Though I was excited to receive the money and the bonus, I was confused because I was not able to count it. Ultimately, having no other option in hand, I decided to leave for my village. I was happy to get the money and happier to go back home. Three months ago, in order to reach here, I had travelled the distance on foot but now I decided to take a bus to my village. Boarding a bus was unusual for me. As soon as I entered the bus, everyone stared at me. At that time, I wasn't able to understand the reason for this kind of behaviour. I felt embarrassed and uncomfortable, so I rushed to the last row and sat down silently. In some time, I forgot whatever happened a few minutes ago.

When the bus started, I looked out of the window out of curiosity. As it moved down the uneven terrain, I saw the hills and lush green forests. There were also colourful flowering plants along the way. For the next two hours, I didn't even look inside the bus. I was lost in the beauty of the surroundings, until the conductor patted my back and informed me that I had arrived at my destination.

The bus dropped me on the main road. In those days, our village was not connected to the main road and we had to walk 6 kilometres down the main road to reach our village. I don't know why that distance of 6 kilometres appeared to be an endless walk that day. I wanted to rush back home, but the last three months had exhausted me and I couldn't walk fast. When I reached home, my mother came running and hugged me. Tears welled up in her eyes. I could feel the pain of separation that she must have felt. She kissed my forehead and looked at me lovingly. In the evening, when my father returned from the farm, I handed over the entire sum of money to him. Unable to control my excitement, I told him to count the notes. To my utter disbelief, the amount was too little. I was just paid Rs 460 instead of Rs 1250 that was promised to me. So, the only good thing to happen as a result of three months of intense hard work didn't turn out to be good either. I felt cheated and so did my father.

I was agonized and aghast that I was misused by someone else. I grew gloomy and morose. Sensing my dejection, my father came up to me and promised me that he would make sure the contractor paid the entire amount. The very next day, my father took me along with the village *pradhan* (head) and two other people to Shimla to meet the contractor. Fortunately, the contractor hadn't left the place and it was easy to locate him. We started off by politely requesting him to give us the remaining amount. The man not only ignored our request, but went on to abuse and show utter disrespect to the villagers. Clearly, he was a cheat and in no mood to pay us. When the villagers realized that this man wouldn't heed their words, they warned him of grave consequences. He then got a little scared and started blabbering. He told the villagers that the rest of the money was spent on the food for the workers. Listening to this, I could stand silent no longer. *'Kuch bhi khane ko nahin deta tha ye* (He never gave us anything to eat),' I told my father, glaring at the man with hatred in my eyes.

He didn't have any other option. He was surrounded by four people, who were ready to teach him a lesson. Ultimately, he agreed to pay and after a lot of negotiations, paid us Rs 600 which my father put in my hands. I was satisfied now. At least, I had earned something in those three months.

Most of the time, in order to earn our bread and butter, we put in all our effort. We try to give it whatever it takes. We exhaust all the energy we have in our bodies. What we expect in return is to lead a better quality of life. Every morning brings with it a number of expectations, aspirations and demands. When those demands are not met or when we are cheated by the people for whom we have worked, it feels like the end of the world. I learnt from this episode that when things go wrong, one needs to stand up for oneself.

5

An Escape

January 1983

Extreme and formidable are the two words that come to my mind when describing the winter in the hills. It is, perhaps, the best time for tourists and revellers as they can dress up in their best winter woollies and enjoy frolicking in the snow. For a casual onlooker who watches people playing in the snow and throwing snowballs at each other amidst laughter and gaiety, it may seem like a lot of fun, but for anybody who has lived in the hills during the harsh winter, the reality is starkly different.

During this time, life comes to an almost complete standstill for the people residing in the mountains. It is especially difficult for the poor, who may not have proper winter clothing, blankets, sufficient food and rations to last them the entire season. The region is draped in a white sheet of snow and the chill becomes unbearable. We never looked forward to winter. Many a time, we have sustained ourselves only on jaggery for days and on some days, we had no food at all. I have spent many such winters in an old suit and a tattered blanket—my only possessions.

Owing to the extreme winter, schools were closed for around two months. It was an extended vacation for my elder brother and cousin. Having nothing much to do, we decided that instead of whiling away our time lazing around at home, we should go out and look for some job and earn money. We contacted a contractor, who informed us about a construction project going on in a place called Jubbal, around 200 kilometres away from our village. A road was being constructed on the outskirts of Jubbal and we were required to help by using explosives to blast the hills and then clean the rubble so that a road could be built there. We were promised Rs 15 a day, an amount considered good in those days. The job seemed easy to me, unlike what I was told to do previously. We agreed to do the job and left for the place.

Being little kids, we were pretty excited about our new job and started doing our work with great enthusiasm and dedication. Since we were too young to do heavy labour, we were told to help the other workers in the blasting process. Things looked good. The contractor was a good man, nice to talk to and quite considerate too. My elder brother's presence also made things easier for me.

But little did I know that my 'easy' days were to be short-lived.

On the third night of our stay, I was rudely awakened by the sting of sharp, cold wind. It was the middle of the night and I was freezing. When I peeped out of the hut, I saw that the entire region was covered in a thick, white blanket. It was snowing! I walked back to where I had been sleeping, pulled my blanket over my body, curled myself into a ball in order to evade the cold and tried to sleep again.

When everyone finally woke up in the morning, the snowfall had still not ceased. The hills were covered in a white blanket and the weather was horrible.

'It won't be possible to work today,' the contractor informed everyone.

That meant no earning for the day. We had little choice other than to sit in the room and wait for the snowfall to cease. But the disappointment aggravated when the snowfall didn't stop even on the second day. It kept snowing for days and everyone got more impatient and gloomy with each passing day. We waited for two weeks, but the weather only worsened. Then, there came a time when we ran out of food supplies and our very survival was in jeopardy. We were starving.

Then, one day, the contractor suddenly told us to leave as quickly as possible. There was nothing we could do about that. When we asked for our wages, we were handed an amount of Rs 50 which was supposed to be shared between the three of us—my cousin, elder brother and I. The remaining amount was deducted for the food that was given to us.

I felt dejected as I stared at the Rs 50 note. All my high hopes suddenly crashed and shattered. When I left the place, there were tears rolling down my face. I felt useless. With no other option, we quietly left the place with almost no money in our hands and our hearts laden with gloom. I felt angry at God. Why didn't He let us work?

Our village was around 200 kilometres away from that place and to cover that distance on foot, in deep snow, without proper clothing and money, was indeed a daunting task. I did not own a pair of shoes and therefore, had no option but to cover the entire distance barefoot.

Here, I want to mention that in my childhood, I never owned a pair of shoes. Till the age of eight or nine, I wore home-made leather slippers. But after that, I could not find any shoes of my size and neither could I afford to wear customized shoes. I got my first pair of slippers at the age of seventeen. My shoe size is eighteen and it was not available in or near my village in those times. So, I spent all my childhood walking barefoot.

I knew that walking for over 200 kilometres was going to be difficult, but it was not until I actually started walking the distance that I realized the level of difficulty. For the initial 20–25 kilometres, the path was covered in thick layers of snow. Initially, only the freezing cold bothered my feet. Then, as I trudged along the snow-covered road, I felt the blood in my veins gradually freezing and with each step I took, I started losing sensation in my feet. I began shivering and my teeth chattered uncontrollably. When I looked down at my palms, I saw that they were losing colour and slowly turning pale green. My legs gave up and refused to carry me forward. Then eventually, I lost sensation in my entire body and I felt numb. When I tried to take another step forward, I fell down on the snow. My chin hit something hard and I felt a searing pain.

For a moment, the world whirled around me and I closed my eyes to stop the dizziness. When I touched my chin with my fingers, I felt something warm splattered across it. As I examined my fingers, I saw a thin stream of blood trickling down my thumb and realized that I had cut my chin. Pulling myself up with a heavy grunt, I pressed my palms over my chin to stop the blood flow. Then, I tore a piece off the cloth

I was wearing and tied it around my face, covering my chin. I started to walk further.

After walking for over 10 kilometres, I stopped. I was exhausted and frozen. But there was no choice. I took a few deep breaths and gathered my strength. I continued walking. I stopped at intervals, rubbed my feet and used my jacket to cover my feet for warmth. Then, finally, after a back-breaking walk over many kilometres, the layers of snow started thinning. The area became relatively less cold. Relieved at the new-found comfort, we continued to walk. We walked throughout the day. At night, we stopped at a roadside dhaba for dinner. But when we looked at the prices and saw that a single plate costs Rs 5, we knew it was well beyond us to spend Rs 15 for a meal. We then decided to buy some jaggery from a nearby shop for Rs 7 and all of us had small lumps of jaggery for dinner. We gave our exhausted bodies rest for a couple of hours at the dhaba, after which we woke up and continued our walk. We walked for the entire second day and though unlike the previous day, the roads weren't buried in thick layers of snow, it wasn't like walking on a bed of roses either. The road that we took was coarse. Stones and small sharp pebbles covered the path and tiny prickly shrubs grew all around it. As we tread along the path, the stones bruised the soles of my feet, and little drops of blood trickled down my feet. I had no alternative but to make a paste from the tree leaves and cover my wounds with it. Every now and then, I stopped because there were also many sharp thorns that pierced through my feet, making it impossible for me to move forward. I then sat down and pulled out those thorns, leaving red scars smeared with blood. The scars were so painful that it felt as if it were the result of numerous ant bites. Ironically, I then longed for the dreadful snow-covered road that I had walked on the previous day. Perhaps, our fate was playing games with us.

We walked for three days, bearing extreme pain and harsh weather with only one thought egging us on—survival! This was one of the most challenging phases of my life, both physically and emotionally. My soul was screaming inside me, yet not a single cry escaped my mouth. I felt forlorn, cheated, anguished and lost. I looked up at the blue sky and wondered if there was a God looking at me, and if there was, why was He not doing anything to help us? I kept gazing at the sky for a long time, asking questions, till my eyes watered. I longed for answers.

Somehow, we finally reached our village. But we had exhausted all our money. It had been a disappointing end to a journey which had been initiated with a lot of hope. Had we completed a full schedule, each one of us would have had more than Rs 500. Now, we had nothing.

When I reached home, I dipped my legs in hot water and salt. It eased my suffering and helped to curb the swelling in my feet.

I never thought that life could be so difficult that there wouldn't be an ounce of comfort left. By now, life had started to teach me different lessons, most of which involved disappointment. Most of the lessons were due to the unexpected setbacks I had to face. However, these incidents made me tough, not just physically but also mentally.

6

Such a Mess

December 1986

With this understanding, I was no longer a child. I became mature and had a better understanding of things than I did in the past. I continued to work at different places. I took over more jobs than I used to do before. I ventured into all kinds of odd jobs—work related to construction of roads, farming, digging mines, collecting pebbles, loading and unloading vegetables and fruits. Sometimes, the employers paid me daily wages but most of the time I was paid after the completion of an entire project. I undertook everything I was offered. My only concern at that time was to earn enough to feed my family and though the wages were never sufficient, it was still money at the end of the day. I made sure that my brothers and sisters got a good education. I didn't want them to be a labourer like me. I did not want them to go through the kind of experiences I had.

Though I accepted different types of jobs because of the urge to earn more money, I had understood by then the importance of getting payment in the form of monthly wages. Whenever I was paid daily wages, I was never able to save much money. On the contrary, when I got the entire money at the end of the contract, I was able to save more.

There was an incident that took place that year, following which I decided to discontinue daily-wage jobs. This was during the winter of 1986. Since there were no jobs to be found in or around our village during that time of the year, we decided to venture out to the Jubbal area again. Though my father suggested that we look for work based on *dihadi* (daily wages) that would earn us around Rs 30 per day, I begged to differ. I was more inclined towards contract jobs as they ensured us better pay. It was a risky affair though. Our payment depended entirely on our capabilities. If we were able to complete the work, we would be earning a lot more but if we failed to do so, we would get nothing. But at that time, I believed in the mantra, 'More the risk, greater is the profit'. I thus stuck adamantly to my decision. In the end, it was decided that my father would go looking for daily-wage jobs while I would search for contract work.

The next day, my father left home with some like-minded villagers and I went my way. There were two more people with me, Panch Ram and Mohan Singh. Mohan was a friend and he was the same age as me. Panch Ram was twice our age. Mohan was a simple and honest boy while Panch Ram was shrewd and notorious for his over-smart ways.

The three of us wandered about in search of work for a few days. Finally, we came across a *lala* (shopkeeper/ businessman) who owned a huge store of jaggery. He had stored large chunks of jaggery during the summer season, a lot of which remained unsold. In the intense heat of the summer, the jaggery had melted on the floor. The winter solidified it. Our job was to clean the floor and remove all traces of jaggery from it. The three of us didn't think that this was a difficult task. We figured it would not take us long to complete the work. Thus, we finalized the deal for Rs 250. It seemed to be a good amount for such a simple job.

We were thrilled not only because we thought that we had tricked the shopkeeper into paying us more for such a simple job but also because we thought we could get our hands on a lot of jaggery for free. We also told the lala to pay us an advance amount because we had no money left with us. Initially he refused, but when we assured him that his work would be done, he paid us Rs 100.

We were hungry as we hadn't had anything to eat since the previous day, so we went to the nearby dhaba and had food. With the rest of the money, we bought some other things of daily use.

We started the work after a while. Initially, we were happy. But the happiness was short-lived as we realized that the work was nowhere close to being as easy as we had imagined it to be. The jaggery was plastered on to the floor. The cold weather had made it hard and tough to scrape. It was like a bed of solid metal pasted on the floor. We tried continuously for three to four hours and managed to scrape off just a little. It was then that we realized why the owner had agreed to pay us Rs 250 for the job. It was proving to be a Herculean task. The little part that we did manage to scrape off the floor was consumed by us to curb our hunger. We tried our best but nothing seemed to work out. When we tried to break it off using a heavy instrument, it got all the more dense. Finally, we gave up! This was the end of all the excitement we felt throughout the morning.

Nightfall arrived, and we had not yet made any progress. We decided to go back to the lala. We were dejected, tired and scared. We sensed that the man would abuse us as we had already spent the entire advance payment in the morning and ended up doing absolutely nothing. We thought of apologizing to him for it and to tell him about our inability to repay the money that we had taken as advance.

I was really tense this time, because I knew that I hadn't done what I had promised. I had already met enough contractors in the past to know that the lala would not let us go without paying him back the advance money. I could judge them easily. They were least concerned about labourers and were only concerned about their work. Even if we did complete the job successfully, we were not appreciated or rewarded, instead we were made to realize our inabilities and the flaws in our work. I was scared and was expecting similar treatment and a really strong reprimand from him.

But every person is not the same. The world is not as cruel as it seems to be. There are people who understand that all of us are human beings and recognize that it is natural to fail. The lala seemed to fall in that category of men (at that time at least). Though he was a little angry initially, he accepted the fact that we had tried our best and so decided to give us another chance. He assigned us a different job. He said that he had an orchard up in the hills where he intended to build a house. But the area was filled with heavy rocks and our job was to break those rocks and make space for the house to be constructed. He agreed to pay us an amount of Rs 100 per day for the job. He also gave us a day's advance. But he also threatened that if we failed to complete the job this time, he would tell his brother, who was a *thanedar* (police officer) to take action against us. This did scare us a little because, being poor and illiterate, we were really frightened of the police. But this time, we were confident that we could do the work as we had already done similar work a number of times before. The place was a few kilometres away from the village. The next morning, all of us reached there and the lala explained to us in more detail about the work to be done. We asked for dynamite to break the large blocks of rocks along with spades, hammers, chisels and other tools. After that, the lala went back to his place and we started our work.

We were glad that there was no one to keep a check on us. Getting a day's payment in advance only exhilarated our spirits. We loitered around the place, talked amongst ourselves and played hide-and-seek among the tall trees. We began the work only around noon, with no tension in our minds.

We started by drilling holes through the bigger rocks using a hammer and a chisel. We then placed dynamite in those holes and tried to blast the rocks. As we were not aware of the correct technique of doing it, it did not work out. Several attempts and failures later, we still could not get it right. Also, it proved to be quite tiresome. Moreover, Panch Ram was acting over-smart and wasn't paying any attention to the work. He kept on loitering around, bossing us around and acting like he was our supervisor.

Then we came up with another idea. We tried to drill a hole under the biggest rock in the middle of the orchard, so that we could take out that rock first. We worked hard for two more hours but it was all in vain. By now, dusk had fallen and we had absolutely zero output. We were totally exhausted and afraid too.

We looked at each other wondering what to do. We were scared to death as the lala could come any time to check the progress and if he saw that we had failed yet again, he would take us to the thanedar. Also, we hadn't earned a penny yet and there was already a debt of Rs 200 on us.

'Let's run away!' Panch Ram came up with the stupidest idea ever. I gave him a stern look and he shut up immediately.

While we were discussing ideas with one another, we saw a man coming towards us. I hadn't seen him earlier, nor had anyone else among us. The man had a thick beard, which looked frightening. Maybe the lala has sent him, I thought.

He came and inquired about us and introduced himself as a rich businessman, who owned lots of apple farms and warehouses. We were told that his distribution network was spread all over Himachal Pradesh, Delhi and some parts of Uttar Pradesh too. He kept on ranting and boasting about himself. He also told us that the thanedar was his distant relative and he wasn't afraid of him and his position. By now, we had understood that this man completely envied the lala and had some sort of rivalry with him. His words were so convincing that we immediately believed him. We told him about our situation.

'The lala is not a nice man. He will hand you over to that devil, the thanedar. The thanedar will beat you brutally and put you behind bars,' he told us.

I was already scared of the police since I had heard stories of what they had done. Numerous incidents of this sort had been narrated to me during childhood and his words further aggravated my terror. I somehow wanted to escape from that place and we all requested him to save us.

'All right, I can give you some work in my apple farm. You would have to do as I say and you will be paid Rs 30 per person per day,' he offered.

'What about the lala? What about the thanedar? What if they came to see us?' Panch Ram asked.

'Huh! I don't give a damn about them. They are nobody to me,' he bragged again.

We were now in a do-or-die situation. The bearded man seemed to be like a messenger of God who had come to save us from the wrath of the lala and the feared thanedar. Without giving a second thought, we went with him.

As I followed the man, I recollected the day I had argued with my father. I hadn't been ready to work for a job which would earn me Rs 30 per day. Now, I was back in a similar job. Had I listened to him and accompanied him, I would have earned a good amount and wouldn't have had to face this misery.

We started work from the next day. We were given a hut to stay at the farm. We observed that the farm had a large amount of scrap. After the bearded man left, we decided to place all the scrap on one side so that we could then take out the small rocks. While I was cleaning the scrap from the farm, an idea struck me.

Scrap is something which could easily be sold! I shared this idea with Mohan Singh and Panch Ram. They liked it and together we decided to collect it and sell it in the nearby market. In accordance with our plan, we began to pile up the scrap on one side of the farm. The only hindrance before us was to carry the scrap to the shop. Panch Ram took the responsibility of getting the sack to put the scrap in. By noon, a big pile was collected and we then waited for Panch Ram to arrive, playing with stones to pass the time. When he brought the sack, we collected the scrap and rushed towards the market before someone saw and stopped us. We earned Rs 50 from the sale. We continued to work there for a few more days.

One morning, we had just started our work when the bearded man came running towards us. He informed us that the thanedar was looking for us and would be there any time. He looked so terrified that he was unable to speak and stuttered.

'Run away from here or . . . or hide somewhere,' he screamed.

We went numb. The very person who had bragged that he wasn't scared of the thanedar was shivering in front of us. We were in a state of shock and terror engulfed all of us. I had already started imagining the scenario wherein the thanedar would arrest us and put us behind bars, but before we could understand what was happening, the thanedar was in front of us.

He had come to look for us based on the lala's complaint. He asked us the reason for leaving the previous job without informing the employer.

We had to give a strong reason in order to save ourselves. I knew that in villages, people were superstitious and believed in spirits and sorcery, so I cooked up a story instantly. I told him that there was an evil spirit there who was guarding that farm, and that spirit did not allow us to break the rocks. I also tried to convince him of the efforts we had put in to get the work finished. I told him further how the spirit had called our names and warned us that if we did not leave the farm immediately, we would be turned into rocks.

The trick worked well. He listened to us calmly and inquired about the money we had borrowed from the lala.

We assured him that the money would be repaid as early as possible. He went away and we heaved a sigh of relief. For the next few days, we worked at the apple farm, earned the required money and repaid the debt.

When we came back home, my father hadn't returned. He came after three days, with a sum of Rs 600 in his pocket. They had collectively earned over Rs 2000 from their daily-wage jobs and other small jobs. When he asked about my earnings, I felt ashamed to tell him that I had come back empty-handed. The disappointment and resentment was so intense that I couldn't stop crying for a couple of days. This was the first and the last time that I had argued with my father. After this, I ensured that whatever I did in life, I would first ask my father for advice. I also gave up my decision of working only for contract-based jobs and understood the importance of working in itself, be it of any kind.

7

One Desperate Attempt

January 1987

As I mentioned earlier, winter in the hilly areas is much more severe than in other parts of the country. It is a tough period not only because of the cold but also due to lack of work. Snow spreads all over the place and it is difficult to undertake any construction work during this time. It had been almost a month since I wasn't able to generate any money. The condition in my home was going from bad to worse. I felt bad to see my siblings crying from hunger. Every day, I went to the nearby areas to look for work. But I came back teary-eyed. The chill was to continue for the next two months. I had to do something to feed my family. None of my family members was able to get any kind of work owing to the same reason.

It is said that the need for food forces a person to do things one hasn't even dreamt of. One day, when I went out looking for a job with a friend of mine, an idea struck me. It was to prepare home-made liquor. This was the time when the consumption of home-made liquor increased greatly. In order to keep the body warm, people often consume alcohol in hilly areas. It not only keeps their bodies warm, but also provides the energy to beat the cold.

Thus, alcohol is an integral part of people's life in these areas. The poor, who do not have money to buy expensive alcohol, prefer to go for home-made liquor. It is prepared from ingredients that are easily available and can thus be made at a very low cost. However, it is difficult to assess the alcohol content in the brew as it is not tested for it. For the same reason, though the production of home-made liquor is prohibited, people still brew it with great secrecy. As soon as I thought about this, the image of my siblings sleeping comfortably flashed before my eyes. I did not think of anything else.

I decided to prepare the home-made liquor known as *sur* among the local residents of Himachal.

I went off into the forest to collect a herb, which was the primary ingredient, after one of the villagers directed me to the place where it could be found. The forest was dense and covered with pine and oak trees, which were so tall that they seemed to touch the skies. There were trees of alder, chestnut, birch and cherry too, and a large number of bamboo trees.

The forest was absolutely still. The occasional chirping of birds and the growl of bears broke the silence. By then, I had walked for a few miles and was in the interior of the forest. The forest got denser. The herbs were in the form of small bushes and were not more than three-feet tall. I had been informed about the appearance of the herb and after searching for some time, I found a small bush that matched the description. I collected the leaves in a sack.

The visit to the forest was quite interesting for me. I wished to stay back in the forest for some more time and sleep comfortably in the lap of nature. The forest had completely captured my imagination. I didn't feel like leaving and going home. I just wanted to enjoy the silence. Also, I was tired after searching for the herb for quite a long time. I thought of resting for some time and lay down near one of the trees for half an hour. The silence of the forest was soothing. I don't remember when I drifted off into sleep.

When I woke up and looked around, I was shocked to find that it was late evening. The night had confiscated the daylight. I was worried and scared. I was frightened as I had heard from my mother about the large number of dangerous animals that wandered in the forest after dusk. My mother had instructed me to come back home before nightfall even if I didn't find the herb. I was also concerned about my mother, who, I knew, must be worried because I hadn't reached home. With every passing minute, it got darker. I left the forest in a hurry. The forest was not alluring for me any more and I missed home. I just wanted to get away from that place as soon as possible. Though it was cold, I was sweating and it took me more than an hour to get out of the forest. I was relieved when I finally reached closer to my village. While I was approaching the village, I saw a large number of people coming towards the direction of the forest. I saw my parents along with a number of other villagers. My mother was in tears and my father had a worried look on his face. The other villagers were trying to console them. As soon as my mother saw me, she ran towards me and slapped me hard. I didn't react or feel hurt as I knew it was my mistake. She held my hands tight and dragged me home. Once home, I was scolded by both my parents and my elder brother for my irresponsible behaviour, but later they calmed down and fed me. All this time, the herb that I had collected from the forest lay on a ledge in the house and no one was concerned about it.

Next morning, I verified whether the herb I had collected was indeed the one that was required for making the liquor. After confirming this, I mixed the leaves with the other ingredients, closed it in an airtight jar and left it untouched for a couple of weeks.

Once the fermenting process was done, I took it out. The stench of the mixture was unbearable and I had to cover my nose with my hand. The smell of home-made liquor is more irksome than that prepared in factories after processing. In our family, nobody consumed liquor. Hence, the smell was far more irritating and infuriating for my family. My mother scolded me for preparing it at home.

Money is important in life. It is required to fulfil one's basic needs. But God is partial when it comes to money. Some can never earn enough money to even afford their daily bread and butter while there are others who earn so much that they can't spend enough of it. It is often said that the need for money makes us do things that we would never have imagined doing and it was just this dire need for money that forced me to prepare that stinking pot of liquor.

So, I prepared about twenty bottles of liquor and then looked for a market where I could sell it. After inquiring from villagers, I went to Ronhaat, which was at a distance of 7 kilometres downhill from my village. Ronhaat was the largest market near our village and people from over seven to eight nearby villages came there to buy things of daily use and all other major household items. The market hosted around thirty to forty shops selling varied commodities and it was more like a fair. There was also a liquor shop in the market, so I expected that there would be a large number of people in and around the place who would be willing to buy my liquor.

When I reached the market, I searched for people who would be willing to be my customers. I kept wandering but was unable to decide how to go about selling the liquor. I wasn't a professional businessman, neither did I have a shop nor any banner which could let people know that some fine home-made liquor was available for sale. I didn't have a bicycle on which I could sit and cycle around the market shouting and promoting my product at the top of my voice. I had a finished product with a non-existent selling mechanism. I asked some people in the market to buy the liquor from me but they simply ignored me without a second thought. However, I did not give up and I kept asking.

Finally, I found a person who took interest in my product. Initially, he asked me for a sample. On tasting it, he appreciated me for making such good liquor. However, he expressed his disappointment by saying that he did not have the money to buy it. I was disappointed but this conversation gave me some confidence to talk to people. I knew that my product was good. I found a few more people in the evening but to no avail. They all asked for the samples and appreciated the product, but when it came to buying it, no one had the money for it.

By evening, I had not earned even a single paisa. In fact, I had spent two entire bottles for sample tasting. I packed the remaining bottles in the sack and went out of the market, with disappointment written clearly on my face. After working for over fifteen days, I hadn't earned even a single penny. I did not want to go back home empty-handed, but I was left with no other option. I climbed uphill, gritting my teeth in sadness and disillusionment.

I moved with slow and halting steps when I saw my tau ji coming from the village. He was the one who had given me the opportunity to work. I greeted him and on his inquiry, I informed him that I had tried to sell liquor but had to go back empty-handed. He said he wanted to taste the liquor. He found it good and decided to buy all the stock. He offered to pay Rs 5 per bottle, which was half the market price. I immediately refused as he was obviously trying to benefit from my situation.

I picked up the bottles, left him and continued walking towards my village. On the outskirts of the village, I spotted Deuru Ram. He was an alcoholic and would drink day and night. Even at that time, he was so drunk that he wasn't able to walk properly. His eyes were completely red and bulged out. Though he was a person we always would try to stay away from, at that point of time, he was the ideal customer for me.

I went up to him and made him taste the liquor. He liked it a lot, appreciated my skills and requested me to give him the entire stock. When he inquired about the price, I told him that I won't sell it at anything less than Rs 10. He accepted the price but the glitch was that he had no money with him at that time. However, on his persistent request, I handed over all the bottles to him. He promised to pay the money within a week. A week later, he still hadn't paid the entire amount. Every time I went up to him asking for my money, he gave me Rs 10 or Rs 20. It took me almost two years to recover the entire payment.

When I look back, I know what I did in desperation at that time was wrong. One should work through hardships, but certain values should never be forgotten.

Meanwhile, I kept doing any work that came my way. I never gave it a lot of thought. I didn't have much of a choice either. Sometimes, I was able to find a job and sometimes I wasn't. Sometimes, my hard work won and sometimes my ill fate. Thus, life went on. I can easily recollect those days when I used to load an entire truck of potatoes for as little as Rs 5. The work was hard; harder than sitting on the roadside and breaking huge rocks throughout the day. Picking up a sack of 100 kilograms on your back, loading it on a truck single-handedly, and that too, hundreds of times in a day, was not an easy task. But I was not in a position to negotiate. Poverty and hunger can make us do anything.

We generally hear or read in newspapers about people dying due to intensive cold or heat. Do you really think heat or cold can kill someone? I don't think so. They die because of poverty. They die because of deprivation.

8

My First 'Real' Job

February 1991

I got the opportunity to work in Rohru, a beautiful, serene town situated on the banks of the Pabbar River on the outskirts of Shimla. This was a town known for its beautiful valleys. The weather was pleasant during the summer and the picturesque valleys were a treat to the eyes. Clouds seemed to float just above your head and it seemed like one could actually reach out and touch them. Quaint little huts were scattered all around the valleys and one could spot little boys and girls with plump rosy cheeks scurrying around with baskets of flowers and fruits. The town was so beautiful that if you visited it once, you would not feel like going back home. I was hired to work for a road construction company, and I enjoyed my work there. The contractors here were more professional than the ones at the village or other places near my village. They appraised the work impartially and paid correct wages to the labourers.

I befriended a few co-workers of my age at the site. Being in the same age group helped as I had good companions to talk to and pass my time with when we were not working. Life was relatively smooth. Though there were moments of discomfort as the job was gruelling in nature, I grew accustomed to it. One day, while I was working at the construction site, a person came to meet me. I had never seen him before. He was well dressed and wore a black suit and white shoes. He was around two-thirds of my height and bulky.

He introduced himself as Giri. He was a businessman who owned a number of restaurants in Shimla and a few other places as well. He said that he had heard about me from a man in a nearby village who worked at his restaurant. That man had seen me working at the site and had told his boss about my towering height and gigantic body structure. During those times, I didn't know my exact height. Though I was aware that I was the tallest person in the whole village, the thought of measuring my height never occurred to me. The gentleman made some general inquiries and said that he was astonished and impressed by my physique. He then asked me if I would be willing to work as his bodyguard. I was taken aback for a moment as I had no idea how to react to this proposal. Soon, I realized that I had nothing to lose except my poverty and deprivation, so I took the obvious decision—I went along with him.

We negotiated for a long time about my salary and after haggling for quite a while, the gentleman finally settled on offering me an amount of Rs 1500 per month. Apart from the basic salary, my food and lodging expenses were also to be paid by him. All I had to do was stay with him and guard him wherever he went.

When I thought about giving this job a chance, doubts crept into my mind and I was apprehensive about my decision. But that very moment, the memory of all those endless nights of poverty and starvation rushed back to me. I was finally getting a permanent job, which was much better than anything I had done before. Moreover, the work didn't seem as exhausting as my previous jobs. I didn't even know what a bodyguard was actually supposed to do. The only thing I understood was that I had to take care of the boss and protect him from any external harm. This seemed like hardly any work and I was being given food, shelter and a good salary for this. What more could I ask for?

I said yes to the gentleman and accepted the job. I had finally found a way in life. I started feeling that things would at last fall into place and I was happy. Giri looked friendly and supportive. Also, this was the first time that somebody had appreciated my physique. Prior to this, my body had always been a subject of crude mockery. From neighbours to friends and co-workers, everybody had made fun of my size and height.

But Giri was different. He told me that I could start my job immediately and that I had to leave with him right then.

That was the first time that I got an opportunity to sit in a car. I was, obviously, ecstatic beyond measure. I ran my hands over the car and a shiver of excitement ran through my body. The white Ambassador looked so appealing that I kept on staring at it for a few minutes. I just could not take my eyes off it. The excitement of sitting in an Ambassador outshone the happiness of getting a permanent job!

As I was getting inside the car, Giri asked me, 'Where are your belongings?'

I looked at him with a straight face and passed a dry smile while gesturing towards the ragged clothes I was wearing—a kurta, pyjama and a scarf with which I wiped the sweat from my body.

'These are the only things that I possess,' I said and sat in the car.

The car began to move towards its destination, and so did my life.

But destiny had something different in store for me. Things were not going to be as easy as they seemed to be at that time. The car had just crossed a hill, when the driver stopped the car all of a sudden. A man had parked his vehicle on the road in such a manner that it was difficult for any other vehicle to pass through. Giri ordered me to get it moved from the way and to abuse the person sitting in that car.

Giri's orders took me by surprise. I did not understand the need to abuse. Things could easily be settled by requesting the man politely to move his car. I told Giri so, but he was adamant and told me to abuse the man and also hit him if need be.

This was something which I didn't like at all at that time. It was the very first day of work and he was unnecessarily bossing me around. Perhaps he wanted to test me. So, I had no other choice than to listen to his orders. I felt frustrated as I had never done this before. I got out of his car and did what Giri ordered me to do. Thankfully, the person concerned moved his car aside as soon as I spoke to him angrily and we set off again. The anguish in my mind withered after a while, but I was still feeling guilty for abusing the man unnecessarily. The joy of getting the new job and sitting in a car slightly diminished.

After two hours, we reached Shimla. I had been to this hilly town numerous times before but the only thing I remembered of this place was the number of rocks I had to break and the roads I had to construct. It was the first time I appreciated and marvelled at the beauty of the town.

The beautiful valleys, the quaint little huts, the greenery, the waterfalls gushing into the rivers and every other beautiful aspect of nature brought joy to me. It also struck me that beautiful things exist to provide pleasure to rich people. We, the poor, never learn to appreciate the beauty of the valleys. We don't have the time to admire and revel in the glory of nature. Even the snow-covered hills, which are a spectacle for tourists, are often mere construction sites for us where we work hard in order to earn money to satiate our hunger.

But then, while travelling in the car, I enjoyed the beauty of Shimla. I loved the lush valleys. I enjoyed watching the towering hills, the sound of gushing rivers, the sound of pebbles being crushed as the car drove over them and the incessant chattering of monkeys—everything was suddenly music to my ears.

Then the car stopped at some point. 'This is my restaurant,' Giri announced proudly and I reached where I was destined to go. Those two hours of the journey seemed to have passed in two minutes as I was lost in enjoying the beauty of the surroundings.

I was in front of a Chinese restaurant. After we entered the restaurant, Giri told me to order anything of my choice. It was the first time that I had a chance of visiting a restaurant and that too, a Chinese one. I had no idea about Chinese cuisine. So, I didn't reply and stayed quiet, and pretended to be interested in observing what was going on in the restaurant. When he asked me again, I told him about my plight. I told him that I would like to eat dal–roti.

To this, Giri started laughing as if I had cracked a joke. For quite a while, I wasn't able to understand why he was laughing. After that he informed me that the restaurant only specialized in Chinese cuisine and that roti and dal weren't served there. I felt myself turning red with shame. He clearly thought that I was a fool for not knowing such things. However, later, dal and roti were specially made for me and I enjoyed a good meal.

By the time the food arrived, Giri and I discussed work. He informed me about his daily schedule—the time at which he woke up, when he went to sleep, the duration for which he remained in his restaurant, the time that was reserved for drinking and the time of his meetings. I just had to be with him like a shadow at all times, to protect him from any kind of mishap.

In a short time, I began to enjoy the job. I enjoyed the comforts, the facilities, the type of work and the better payment. I no longer needed to pick up huge sacks, blast hills or break heavy rocks. The work of a bodyguard seemed to be nothing compared to the exhausting manual labour I had done before. I was getting proper sleep and a proper three-meals-a-day diet. On my part, I tried my best to ensure that I worked according to Giri's will and made every effort to impress him.

After about a week into the job, two men came to take my body measurements. On inquiring about the reason, they told me that I would be provided a bodyguard's uniform. I will be getting a uniform. Wow! I was on cloud nine. This was the first time in my life that I was given the chance to wear proper attire. I always wore a kurta, with pyjamas or a trouser. Even these were ragged as I could never afford the luxury of new clothes.

Another week later, I was given a black shirt and a pair of trousers of the same colour along with a pair of slippers. I was overjoyed to see my uniform. I quickly went to my room and changed. I checked myself in the mirror several times from every possible angle. For the first time in my life, I admired my body and fell in love with myself. Such a great feeling it was! I was happy.

Giri told me that I looked stunning and professional. 'You look so intimidating that people will think twice before approaching you,' he added. I thought I looked younger in the uniform and that it added perfection to my appearance as a bodyguard.

Giri was born with a silver spoon in his mouth. His father had been one of the richest businessmen of the city and had left him a huge property. But I never understood what he did exactly, apart from travelling from one city to another, and boasting about his money, power and authority. Giri also had a bad drinking habit. Sometimes, under the influence of alcohol, he didn't even realize who he was talking to. Many a time, he lost control, swore and abused people. He pretended to be a daring person but I could sense that he was a coward at heart.

Once when Giri got really drunk, he got into a brawl with another man. That man also had two well-built bodyguards accompanying him. I tried to intervene and talk them out of the situation but Giri and the other man were too drunk to even listen to what I was saying. They abused and swore at each other. The situation got serious and then suddenly, the other man told his bodyguards to hit Giri. Before anyone could lay hands on my boss, I jumped into action and single-handedly shoved the two bodyguards out of Giri's way, landing hard punches on their jaws. One of them broke his jaw in the impact and screamed in pain, holding his bleeding chin. Seeing this, his boss got scared and ran off with the two men. I held a drunk and wobbly Giri in my arms and carried him safely away from the scene before the police could intervene.

However, this was just the beginning. Such events became recurrent. Every other day, Giri used to involve himself in a number of verbal fights which quickly turned physical. I always remained at his side and on my guard so that I could handle the situation before it turned ugly.

Because of this, a number of people began to recognize me. I found that many people started appreciating and admiring my physique and power. The people who had seen me fight during the brawl were hesitant to indulge in an argument with Giri as they feared me.

I felt powerful and respected. But this was my misconception. In reality, I was a subject of mockery for many. People looked up to me, not out of admiration, but out of surprise. For them I was nothing more than a seven-foot-tall giant they were scared of. However, I didn't care about it at this stage.

Giri told me about the people he didn't like and how they needed to be taught a lesson. I started taking a keen interest in his affairs. I was a changed man. Even before I realized it, I was slipping into darkness. I didn't have to be ordered to utter abusive words or slap someone. I was now getting used to hitting, beating and thrashing people. I even got involved with a few local gangs.

As a result of these activities, I suddenly had a number of enemies. Every second day, I was involved in a fight. I started enjoying the fights. I had no control over my hands. Power had completely corrupted my heart and mind. Whenever I hit anyone, it gave me immense pleasure and I felt victorious after defeating them. It made me feel like the king of the world. I started seeing these episodes as adventures in my life and I wanted more and more of these.

Whosoever came to visit my boss talked about my height and size. They often asked me about my family and the place

I belonged to. I answered them but I didn't realize then that their inquisitiveness came from their desire to know the reason behind my extraordinary size.

I was happy and satisfied with my job. I no longer struggled to sustain my life. The basic needs of life—food, clothing and shelter—were getting fulfilled quite easily. Above all, the authority and the power that came with the job made me feel invincible.

But soon, things turned around for the worse. Once, I got involved in a personal fight with some people and Giri's helpers told him about it. The same evening, I overheard Giri speaking to his wife about me. He abused me and said that I always got involved in fights. He further blamed me for getting entangled in useless issues and for degrading his social status. I was shocked as I had always considered Giri to be a person who supported me wholeheartedly. But it was only now that I realized that he wasn't a man to be trusted. He appreciated me on my face and abused me behind my back. This kind of behaviour revealed his arrogance and showed that he was self-obsessed. I understood that he considered me as nothing more than a slave. It was as if I didn't have any rights or emotions of my own. Suddenly, I understood how I had compromised my humanity, blinded by power and authority. I realized how I had forgotten who I was and under the influence of Giri had slowly become like him.

For some time after that incident, I felt like leaving my job. What was the meaning of working for someone who did not respect me? What was the meaning of compromising one's morals for such a person? I questioned myself constantly. I knew that if I needed Giri's support during a conflict instigated by him, he would definitely abandon me and blame me as the culprit. He wouldn't think twice before back-stabbing me. Once I realized this, I couldn't shake off this thought. I wanted to leave the job desperately, but then I didn't have any other option. However, I didn't want to go back to my previous life of instability where not even a single day's payment was guaranteed. I had to support my parents and also ensure that my brothers' and sisters' education continued without any hindrance. I didn't want anyone to suffer just because I wasn't happy with my job. I curbed my thoughts and decided to continue working.

But this was a mistake. I was going to face the agony of not leaving for home in the next few days.

9

Fights outside the Ring

December 1991

It was the last evening of the year. The excitement of New Year filled the cold air of Shimla. The fairy lights on the snow-covered apple and pine trees dazzled like a million stars in the dark. The roads were blanketed in thick sheets of snow and peppered with colourful balls and ribbons. The city was dressed like a beautiful bride and its beauty was mesmerizing. The people further added to its beauty by putting up incandescent lights that glowed all over the city. The light snowfall made the entire place look surreal, as if it was straight out of a fairy tale.

A walk on the Ridge Road of Shimla to the Christ Church and the library was an enchanting experience. A grand feast had been arranged at every pub, bar, discotheque and restaurant. In addition to this, people had congregated in open areas and were preparing bonfires. There was excitement in every corner.

A few of my friends and I also decided to explore the city on foot and welcome the new year. We went out to the Mall

Road, which was the busiest street of Shimla even then. We were there, when all of a sudden, a group of boys came—most of them heavily drunk. This group included some students who rambled around, created a commotion, passed rude comments at the passers-by and disturbed the peace of the town.

They told me to come along with them and enjoy the night the way they wanted to. I refused. I politely told them that I had my own set of friends and that I couldn't possibly abandon them. All of a sudden, one of them held my hand and pulled me forcefully. I hated his brash behaviour. Unable to control my sudden burst of anger, I punched him hard on his face. The impact was so brutal that he immediately fell to the ground. The other men looked at me in shock. For a few seconds, none of them said anything. Perhaps, they were too frightened.

Before they could do anything, I asked, 'Does anyone else want to get their teeth broken?'

There followed a deathly silence. The only thing they did was to run away. I was furious. I could feel that I was becoming a slave to my anger but it was beyond my control. I didn't have any fear at that moment of time. Neither of them nor of the police!

By that time, I had built quite a reputation in the valley. My ideas of power and authority were deluded. The people in the valley were scared of me. My power, might, courage and punches increased their fear. I felt exuberant and confident. I felt that no one in the valley was more powerful than me. I felt a high by the effect a single punch of mine had created and walked back with my head held high. My friends also felt proud of me.

We kept roaming on the Mall Road. I felt as if I was the 'king' who had all the power of the world in his hands. I could do anything. It wouldn't be wrong to say that a sense of pride had completely taken over my wisdom and morals. Within a few minutes, we forgot about the incident and began to enjoy the scenery.

Night was now approaching and the city was at its best. Numerous lamps were lit up and fairy lights were burning bright across the streets. Both the open areas and the pubs were getting crowded with people coming in from all over. The dim moonlight falling on the ice-capped hills only added to the beauty.

Music emanated from every pub and restaurant. All the shops, departmental stores and restaurants that usually closed by that time were open to welcome the year. All eyes were fixed on the Ghantaghar, a huge clock tower situated near Christ Church, to watch the clock strike twelve. It was 10 p.m. and the enthusiasm was everywhere.

Walking along the road, we reached the Scandal Point, the highest point of the city. From there, the view of the valleys and the mountains was spectacular. My gaze stopped over a hill. It looked beautiful. The faded moonlight falling on it partially illuminated the snow. I felt delighted and refreshed. I was hypnotized by this view and kept staring at it without even turning my face away for a second. Had my friends not taken me out of my reverie and told me to leave, I would have stayed there for the entire night gazing at its beauty.

Moving further, we stopped on the way to the Kali Bari Temple. I was a devotee of Kali Maa and this temple was an abode of Shyamala, an embodiment of Goddess Kali. I believe that my strength and my physique are a gift of Kali Maa. The temple was also illuminated with candles. In order to reach the temple, one had to walk down the Mall Road and climb down the stairs leading to the temple. I left my friends and went down to visit the temple. I had just crossed the very first step when someone pushed me. Though I tried to balance myself and prevent myself from falling, I couldn't and I tumbled down the stairs. My head hit a stone step and it started bleeding. For a moment, I could not understand what had happened. When I looked up, I saw about twenty to twenty-five people advancing towards me. They were in a large group while I was all alone. They also carried an array of objects with them—sticks, bats, chains and much more.

For a second, I thought of retreating and running away. But then, my instinct stopped me. Never in my life had I given up and I was not going to do it then either. In the next second, they surrounded me. I tried to get up, but suddenly someone kicked my face. Pain rushed through my nerves. A man dragged me by my feet. Then I heard the sound of a cloth being torn. One of them had ripped off my collar. I looked about for my friends, but they were nowhere around. Somehow, I gathered my strength and got up. By now, I had been hit so many times and was in so much pain that any other blow would not have had any effect on me.

As soon as I got up, I grabbed one of them and threw him over the others. I don't know how but I was able to revive my strength. One after the other, I grabbed them and hit them hard. I didn't stop even after that. They were also beating me, but it was as if I was immune to pain. I held one guy and beat him up. Blood streamed out of his nose and he dropped to the ground. But this didn't affect me. I was full of anger and nothing would make me stop. I grabbed another person and threw him down and kicked him vigorously. I punched the person standing next to him hard on his back. Scared at seeing me in a destructive rage, the others scurried off in fear.

Bleeding badly, I walked down the stairs, hoping to find a familiar face somewhere. I slowed down after a while and sat down on one of the chairs in an open-air restaurant that was on the path to the temple. After a minute, I felt a hand on my back. It was the waiter of the restaurant. He knew me well. He helped me to go to a nearby tap and I washed my face. This didn't help at all. Blood was still streaming from my head. He told me to sit on the chair and went to talk to the restaurant manager. By that time, I had started feeling intense pain. The manager took me to the nearby hospital. After examining my wounds, the doctor immediately gave the required medical aid and my head was covered with bandages.

But I was least concerned about my wounds. The only thing on my mind was to find out the identity and the whereabouts of the people responsible for it. They were certainly from the same group of boys who had meddled with me in the evening. They looked like they were part of the same gang. I wanted to look for them and avenge the pain I was going through. I left the hospital after some time and immediately began to look for those people. But I wasn't able to find them; instead, I spotted my friends near a pub. I went and narrated the whole incident.

As we walked out of the pub, we encountered two men who were pestering people, passing lewd comments, and cracking vulgar jokes. They didn't seem like local residents and their accent made it clear that they were from Punjab. I was walking away from the pub with my friends when suddenly one of them pushed and taunted me.

I overlooked his comments and didn't pay attention to him. However, when he passed the same comment again, it aroused my anger. I lost my calm and all the pent-up anger towards those people who had beaten me up earlier was directed towards this man. I caught him, grabbed him by his collar and then slapped his face, not once, not twice, but till he trembled and his facial appearance changed. After pausing for two seconds, I hit him again and again without restraint till he was unconscious. I stopped only when my friends pulled me back and in order to avoid being hauled up by the police, we ran off leaving the man behind.

It was 11.30 p.m. by then and after this incident, we thought of going to a discotheque in order to lighten the mood. I had never been to a discotheque before and hence I didn't have a clear idea about the place except for the things my friends had told me. I just knew that there would be loud music and we were supposed to dance to it. At that moment, I needed something to divert my mind and music and dance seemed to be the perfect alternative.

But this was not the end of the episode. I wouldn't get the liberty to divert my mind. Something far more unpleasant was about to happen. We had already been through a couple of mishaps that day and were in no mood to handle any more violence. But God had some other plans. When we were at the entry gate of the discotheque, a bouncer stopped us, saying that we were not allowed inside as stag entry (single entry without a female partner) was not permitted. My friend requested the bouncer a number of times to allow us to go inside. The bouncer then pushed my friend and slapped him on his face. I couldn't tolerate this unjust treatment. I attacked him. The bouncer fell on the ground and broke two of his teeth. I bent down to hit him again.

Before I could raise my arm and throw my fist at his face again, I heard a cry of pain. It was none other than my friend. A few men had stabbed him with a knife. For a moment, I was in a state of shock. I leapt towards him to cover him up and caught him in my arms. I soon felt a sharp knife being pushed into my left thigh. I screamed loudly and was in terrible pain. All I could remember after that, except the tremendous pain, was the sight of those cowards running away. The pain was excruciating and I felt as if I could not breathe for some time. I fell to the ground and my friend lay beside me in a pool of blood. In the wintery night, I stopped feeling cold and started sweating profusely. The wound made it impossible to get up. Just as the pain became intolerable, I heard the siren of police vehicles in the distance.

Now the policemen will catch me, I thought with fear because I knew that I had been a part of the violence. If I had any strength left with me, I would have escaped from the place. But before I could think further, the cops were upon us. I was pulled up by two policemen and taken to the police station. My friend was taken in an ambulance. At the police station, they interrogated me as they thought I was the culprit. They recorded my statement. I explained the sequence of incidents from the beginning to the end and also that the fight had been initiated by the bouncer. After that, I was taken to the hospital.

I was in a hospital for the second time the same day. In one's life, a person fears and stays away from three places—the police station, hospital and court. I had already had my taste of two in one day.

While we were entering the hospital, I came across the two guys I had thrashed earlier in the evening. They were scared to death on seeing me as they thought I had come there to beat them again and they hurriedly fled away from the hospital.

I was taken to the emergency room. I was made to rest on a bed while the policemen talked to the doctor and the nurses. I thought that I would receive some kind of treatment, but contrary to my expectations, I saw another police inspector coming towards me. He accused me of getting into a fight and warned me that he would put me behind bars if they received any more complaints against me. He commented on my looks and told me that I looked like a criminal. He told me to cut my long hair. I did not like this judgemental comment. The continuous questioning made me feel dejected. His lack of empathy and understanding hurt me more than my wounds. He was hardly concerned about my injuries. Finally, after the intervention of the doctor, the cop moved away, not before warning me once again to not get involved in any kind of fight.

The doctor turned out to be as insensitive as the policeman. He started stitching my wounds without giving me any anaesthetic. I cried out in pain. Every single stitch was so painful that it made the pain from the knife wound seem better. The agony continued for the next twenty minutes and the pain lasted for the entire night. I kept on moaning and was not able to sleep even for a second.

So, New Year's Eve ended with excruciating pain.

Next morning, I was discharged from the hospital. What a way to start the first day of the year!

However, I got the time to reflect on what had happened. The previous night had been excruciatingly painful, but it acquainted me with a different shade of life. Even if it was a bad experience, it was an experience of survival. Life is unpredictable. Even if we wish to control it, sometimes our lack of wisdom and ego blinds us. I realized that there were numerous moments in life when we had to control our anger to avoid aggravating a situation. We need to maintain our calm. We will meet different kinds of people in our lives, who may at times act inappropriately, but if we go on beating up each one of them, there will be no difference between us and them. From that day on, I learnt how to avoid these kinds of people, to tackle difficult situations and also to keep my cool.

10

The Turning Point of My Life

Life is a journey of uncertainties. We never know when a surprise awaits us; one that can turn our entire life upside down and rewrite our destiny completely. There was something waiting for me as well—something which a person, who does a twelve-hour job, eats three square meals a day and lives an ordinary life with meagre possessions, can never think of. Something that was unconceivable for a person who was a poor labourer in the past and a dissatisfied bodyguard in the present.

It was a normal day like any other. I was moving through the hall of Giri's house when I saw a man enter through the gates. He held a camera in one hand and some files in the other. I hurried to the door to inquire about him before he could enter. The man beamed on seeing me and said that he had come to meet me and not Giri. He was a journalist and worked with a leading newspaper in town. He wanted to interview me. I was flabbergasted.

'My interview?' I asked. 'What for?' For a moment, I thought he was joking.

'Because you are different from others. You are huge . . . very huge! Don't you think people should get to know about you?' he asked me.

He further added that he had decided to publish an article about me in their paper. I didn't know how to read newspapers but I had always been awed by them. The colourful advertisements always appealed to me.

This would be great. Now people would see my photograph like I do of others. I will be treated like a star, I thought.

He told me that all I had to do was answer a few questions. So, he began. He asked me about my past life and my journey from being a poor labourer in a small village to being the bodyguard of an influential person in town. I enjoyed bragging about myself. I told him how my gigantic physique was my biggest strength. I told him how I was proud of the impact of my punches and how I beat up many nuisance makers with my powerful hands.

I was extremely elated after the interview. The mere thought of getting an article about me published in a newspaper sent thrills of excitement through my entire body. Never in my wildest dreams could I even afford to imagine a scenario like this.

I was a common man and a common man isn't allowed to dream big. A common man is not supposed to rise up from his anonymity to the heights of popularity. The only thing society expects him to do is earn his daily bread and butter. All that he can do is look for happiness in the gloominess enveloping him because all his dreams are killed even before their inception. But then, there are those rare moments when one of these ill-fated lives manages to rise from mediocrity like a phoenix from the ashes.

The interview was published in the newspaper. In a gradual turn of events, my life was about to change. God had finally decided to wave his magic wand. Without any prior indication, my fate was about to make the most important move in the game called life.

I was excited about showing the article to everyone around me. For the next couple of days, there was a huge crowd outside Giri's house. They seemed excited to meet me and got pictures clicked with me. Everyone expressed their admiration for me and my physique. I was suddenly the centre of attraction and I felt like a celebrity for the first time in my life. I thoroughly enjoyed the attention I got. The fact that Giri was out of town during this time was an added advantage as there was no one there to reprimand or abuse me for the commotion outside the house.

By this time, it had been three months since I had started working as a bodyguard. I had been away from home for a long time and missed it terribly. I had earned a good sum of money by now and was yearning to share the happiness of my new-found celebrity status with my family. Moreover, I didn't have much work as Giri was out of town. So, I called up Giri and told him that I would be leaving for home for a few days.

Meanwhile, another interesting twist of fate awaited me. While I was away from town, the IG (inspector general) of Jalandhar, Chopra*, came to know about the newspaper article featuring my interview. He got to know this through another colleague of his, Ramesh*, who was the DSP (deputy superintendent of police) of Jalandhar.

---

* Names have been changed to protect privacy.

Chopra, along with Ramesh and the sports secretary of the Punjab Police, Pratap Singh*, decided to find me. They believed that a person of my height and physique had a great future in sports and could do wonders. They planned to recruit me into the Punjab Police department. They wanted people who had a fair idea of the town in their team in order to aid them in their search. There was a police officer, Rakesh, who belonged to Solan, a district close to Shimla. Hence, they sent Rakesh on my search and a senior officer called Ram Chander accompanied him. Unfortunately, that was the time when both Giri and I were out of town and hence could not be contacted personally. So, they talked to the helpers in Giri's restaurant and left word with them.

It was not long before I got back to work and as soon as I returned, I was informed that a couple of policemen had come looking for me. I went pale with fear. The helpers further added that the two officers belonged to the Punjab Police and that they were going to come back. I was terrified. The face of the men I had mercilessly thrashed on New Year's Eve flashed before my eyes. Somehow, I was certain that the police had come to arrest me in that regard and sweat trickled down my panic-stricken face.

A few days later, two men came to Giri's restaurant to meet me. They were dressed in casuals and one of them had a turban covering his head. They introduced themselves as officers of the Punjab Police and informed me that their IG wished to meet me.

I observed the two men carefully and decided not to fall for their make-believe story. In fact, I refused to believe that they were policemen at all since, according to me, a policeman

---

* Name changed to protect privacy.

was always dressed in a khaki uniform. And here they were, standing before me in casuals.

'You think I am an illiterate fool to fall for your made-up story?' I bellowed at them. 'Get yourselves out of the compound right now or you'll be sorry for your entire sad lives,' I said.

I had clearly scared them. But soon, they calmed down and tried to approach me gently. They fished out their identity cards and showed them to me. I did not bother to even look at those since it made no difference and I knew that every second person in the world could forge such a card.

Then, one of them, who had introduced himself as Rakesh, mentioned that he was from Solan and tried to convince me that they were real policemen and weren't trying to fool me in any manner.

I calmed down a little. Rakesh and the other policeman tried again to reason with me. They told me that the IG was looking for me after reading my interview in the newspaper and that they were interested in recruiting me into their department. I was still apprehensive about the credibility of their story. The conversation continued for over an hour where they tried everything to convince me. Gradually, I began to take them seriously. I also realized that these people had no idea about the New Year Eve's incident and so I was safe.

In the end, when I was thoroughly convinced, I agreed to accompany them to Jalandhar the very next day. They told me to meet them at the bus stand, early next morning.

In the evening, I narrated the entire incident to my friends. All of them expressed the initial apprehension I had felt. They told me that all this must be a ploy to trap me. It was quite possible that the Punjabi men from the New Year Eve's incident had set out to kidnap me by sending their men disguised as policemen. Otherwise, why would the Punjab

Police want to recruit an ordinary man from Himachal? There was no logic behind it.

Though I was confident about my ability to protect myself in case anything happened, I could not deny the fact that my friends' doubts made me a little wary too. I had no answer to most of their questions. My instinct told me that they were right. In the end, with tides of confusion still swirling through my mind, I decided not to go.

The next morning, when the two men waited for me long enough at the bus stand and I did not turn up, they realized that I had managed to bluff them. They came to me later that day and contrary to what I had expected, they were calm and decided to listen to all my doubts and fears patiently. They then explained to me why they required me in their sports department. They told me that a man of my height and build would prove to be a valuable member in their team and I had no reasons to be scared of anything.

Finally, after making sure that I would meet them the next morning at the guest house they were staying at, the two men left.

I sat there perplexed and in a daze. A lot of arguments and counterarguments were going on in my mind. Finally, to get a clearer picture, I decided to call up my boss and take his advice. Giri was in Gujarat and when I narrated the entire incident to him and explained my dilemma to him, he did not pay any attention to my problem. As expected, he carelessly told me to take a decision on my own.

Having no other choice, I decided to just close my eyes and think about it quietly. I knew I had to finally listen to my heart. I mentally tried to list all the pros and cons involved in the decision. If they were telling the truth, I was certain that this would be my biggest opportunity in life. Secondly, I knew that Giri was the kind of man I could not completely trust. He could back-stab me any time for his personal gain and I could not see myself working for such a man forever. Moreover, the risk involved was little for the massive opportunity I was being provided with. If at all the entire thing was a sham and I was being tricked, I knew I could escape from it. But if all this was real, then I could not afford to miss this opportunity for anything in the world.

That night, I packed all my belongings into a neat bundle. The two policemen spent the night at the guest house near Giri's home, afraid that I might trick them again. In the morning, I went to the guest house and stood at the entrance. Ram Chander, one of the policemen, smiled on seeing me. But something about him seemed different. Then I noticed that he had not put on his turban. This struck me as unusual since a sardar is always supposed to cover his head with a turban. Ram Chander even had his hair cut short unlike most sardars who never cut their hair. My sceptical mind began forming doubts all over again. All of a sudden, on an impulse, I turned around and left the guest house. I shared my doubts with my friends. They repeated all the same warnings of the previous day. I got highly frustrated now. Making up my mind seemed an impossible task with all the dilemmas in my mind.

Finally, when nothing seemed to clear my doubts, I went back to Ram Chander and asked him blatantly why he was not following the rules of Sikhism. He smiled at my naive question and explained that all sardars do not follow the practice of wearing a turban and not cutting their hair religiously. I listened intently but was still not completely convinced.

Meanwhile, another idea struck me. I told the two policemen that I first needed to visit my home to inform my parents and pack some clothes and money for the journey. Ram Chander then told Rakesh to go along with me while he would head back to inform the IG about the change of plans. Thus, Rakesh and I boarded the bus and headed off to my village. The bus dropped us at the edge of the hill from where it was a 7-kilometre walk uphill to my village. Having been used to this way of living, the walk did not strain me much, but poor Rakesh was hardly able to breath after reaching midway. He had never walked for such a long distance on an uphill terrain and this was evident from his condition. We reached a little further up, when we came across the village pradhan. I greeted him and introduced him to Rakesh. Rakesh explained to him his purpose of visit and told him that he would require a character certificate of me in order to process the recruitment form. The pradhan became excited on hearing the news and gladly agreed to issue a stamped certificate as soon as we reached the village. We thanked him and headed home.

By the time we reached home, Rakesh was completely exhausted. On the contrary, I felt more excited and energetic. I was welcomed by the happy faces of my family members. I introduced Rakesh to them and told them everything about my new opportunity. Everyone was really happy and did not cease thanking Rakesh continuously.

The next morning, I packed some clothes and my father handed me a sum of Rs 2500 for my stay in Jalandhar. This was the same amount that I had given to him during my last visit. He had not spent a single penny from it but had saved everything for me. I was speechless. I refused to take the amount but my father insisted. I finally had no option but to take it.

Soon, it was time to leave. It was difficult to say goodbye to my family. This time, I was leaving my family to venture into a new state altogether. My family was worried and their feelings were expressed in the form of tears. My mother could not stop crying and kept insisting that I must take care of myself and be safe. I promised her that I would.

For parents, their children never grow up, and always remain their little ones, no matter what their age is. I didn't understand it then, but I realize it now when I have my own child. Every second moment, be it during a fight or an event, I think about my daughter. When I am out of home and I call my wife, I cannot hang up without listening to her giggles. That's the kind of love parents have for their children.

Having collected the character certificate from the village pradhan, Rakesh and I left the village and walked downhill to board the bus to Paonta Sahib. From there, we took another bus to Chandigarh. When the bus entered Chandigarh, I looked out of the window and noticed flat plains all around. There were absolutely no hills or valleys. Having never come across anything of this sort before, I squirmed a little in my seat out of a strange worry. When the bus stopped at the stand, I found myself hesitating to get down. Seeing this, Rakesh tried to quell my fears and informed me about the different types of landscapes and that not all areas have mountains and valleys. Some places have plains, plateaus and even stretches of desert.

I was dumbfounded by this new piece of knowledge. I never knew that there were different types of landscapes in the world. I had always spent my life nestled among the hills. There was another major difference in the new place and that was the number of people I spotted. Every few minutes, a bus would halt and people would tumble out of it like flocks of sheep, pulling and pushing each other. Even the buses were of various types. There were the rickety, old ones like the one we boarded and then there were the fancy ones with black-tinted windows and cushioned seats. Everything was so new to me that it was making me a little uneasy.

Then, Rakesh informed me that as our next bus was not scheduled to arrive for another hour, we could finish our dinner by that time. I followed him to a nearby dhaba where we sat down to have dinner. By the time we had finished, our bus for Jalandhar arrived and was already half occupied. Rakesh and I quickly grabbed seats for ourselves and waited for the bus to start and in the next thirty minutes, the bus was crammed with people. In fact, the number of people standing and holding on to the metal bar from the ceiling was more than the number of people seated. It soon became suffocating and congested, so much so that I felt warm even though it was winter. The shrill voices of middle-aged, talkative women and little children wailing loudly only added to my irritation. There were also four policemen with guns. Punjab, in those times, was suffering from a wave of terrorism.

There was one particular incident during that journey that made me rethink about the plight of ordinary human beings. A group of people tried to get on to the bus but were unable to do so since it was already jam-packed. These people who were trying to get in forcefully stopped the bus and some of them climbed on to the roof of the bus. It could have been dangerous to travel like that and that too, at that hour of the night. Somebody could have easily fallen down and met with a ghastly accident. The four policemen got down from the bus and ordered those men to get down from the roof, but their orders fell on deaf ears. When they did not come down from the roof even after being repeatedly told, the policemen dragged them down and beat them. It was later that we came to know that those men were teachers and they had forced themselves up on the bus because they were not getting any transport at that odd hour of night. They only wished to reach home.

In our country, people often face similar problems. They are forced to commit mistakes and when caught, they are beaten and punished. What crime did the teachers commit? Was it a crime that they wanted to reach their homes and this was the only bus available? Had there been any other option available, they would never have gone against the rules. Who wants to sit on a running bus's roof and put one's life in danger? The policemen were also not wrong. They were doing what they were supposed to do. It was part of their duty. In case they had allowed the teachers to sit on the roof and any of them had met with an accident, the people would have held the policemen responsible. The truth is it's not the people who are wrong every time; many a time, their circumstances force them to act in a wrong manner.

After this drama, the bus finally moved again. Having soon forgotten about the incident, other thoughts pressed my mind. I asked Rakesh all sorts of questions about the police department, the city of Jalandhar, the culture of the state and so on. An unsettling feeling of nervousness mixed with excitement overcame me. For the past few days, my life had been moving at such a fast pace that I found it overwhelming to cope with it.

We reached Jalandhar early next morning. Instead of heading straight to the police station, Rakesh took me to his home. His house was a tiny little place with two rooms and five members. Everyone was cordial to me and I felt welcomed. After having some rest, followed by breakfast, Rakesh went off to the police station to report his arrival while I stayed back. My stay at Rakesh's house turned out to be among one of the most special memories of my life. The family was so good to me right from the beginning. They made a persistent effort to make me feel at ease. They included me in all their conversations and made it a point to ensure that I felt comfortable among them. They even took pains to inquire about my favourite food items and prepared them for me. They took care of a stranger in a way not many do and I have been forever grateful to Rakesh and his family for this gesture.

In the evening, Rakesh informed me that I was to report at the IG's office the next day.

What did the next morning have in store for me? Would it be a magic spell which would change my life? Would my life take a turn from that moment? Or would I have to go back to my old life? The answers to my questions floated in the darkness of the night, waiting to be answered with the arrival of dawn.

I woke up before the crack of dawn. Rakesh's mother prepared a delicious breakfast after which we made our way to the Punjab Armed Police (PAP) headquarters where Chopra was waiting for us.

When he saw me, Chopra beamed at me and got up from his chair excitedly.

'This is the man I have been waiting for! Bravo!' he exclaimed. He was extremely happy to see me. I was a little puzzled because I could not exactly fathom the reason for his excitement. This was the man who held one of the highest positions in the police force, and there he was, beaming with excitement to have me in the team.

Chopra was an impressive man. He had an attractive baritone and a posture that only an officer could possess. He spoke in a manner that immediately commanded respect and everything that he said was motivating for the people around him. All in all, he had an appealing personality.

After a brief talk with the IG, I was introduced to Ramesh. He was the one who had first seen the article with my interview and intimated the IG about it. The two men talked to me for over an hour and told me about the department and its way of functioning. At the end of the discussion, they said they would offer me any role of my choice in the department.

Being the uneducated person that I was, I had absolutely no idea about the ranks in the police force. To me, every man in a khaki uniform was the same. I could not differentiate a constable from an inspector. I felt bad and helpless at this point of time.

Everything that was happening seemed like a dream to me. However, different kinds of thoughts cropped up in my mind. Will I be able to do the job? Will I live up to their expectations? What will be the output of the job? How will I manage everything with no knowledge about the work?

'Give me any role of your choice,' I finally told them.

Chopra discussed this with the sports secretary and they decided to offer me the job of a constable. This was the lowest position in the department hierarchy.

This was the second time that I had missed an opportunity because I was uneducated. At this moment, if I had been educated, I could have easily grabbed a better position. It was following these setbacks that I realized the value of education.

Chopra ordered Rakesh to get a tracksuit and boots of my size made. After this, he told me to come to the staff hostel where he introduced me to the hostel authorities, who seemed visibly amazed on seeing my size and build.

He told them to order a special bed for me on which I could sleep comfortably. He also ordered for a special diet to be prepared with extra quantity of food to meet my nourishment needs.

'It will take some time to get everything ready for you. Till then, you can stay at Rakesh's house. Also, in the meantime, get prepared for this job. The role of a policeman is difficult. You need to ensure that everything goes smoothly. You need to get ready to face lots of problems and difficulties. The life of a policeman is not easy, contrary to what common people think. I know it will take some time for you to be prepared, but try to learn things as fast as possible,' Chopra said to me.

He also gave me some money in advance, so that I could get all the commodities for my daily needs. By then, I had become comfortable with Rakesh and his family. They were caring and I liked spending time with them. Rakesh's mother was a great support. She washed my clothes and took care of me as if she was my real mother.

My practice started from the very next day. It was one of the most important days of my life—something I wish to recollect over and over again. When I entered the PAP sports ground in the morning, everyone greeted me respectfully. Everyone tried to talk to me and seemed interested in discussing my unique physique. They wanted to know how I came to have such an astounding physique.

I have quite a few memories of those days. I was naive and in fact, foolish too, if I tell you honestly. Rakesh had a scooter at that time on which we used to ride back to his home. One day, while coming out of the sports ground, he told me that my tracksuit was ready and he would collect it from the tailor. He told me to wait for some time at the exit gate of the sports complex.

I nodded and kept waiting there for a long time. More than an hour passed but Rakesh didn't show up. I thought he might have forgotten to pick me up. By then, I knew the route to Rakesh's home, so I decided to walk to his house. His house was around 6 kilometres away from the sports ground, a distance that was negligible for me as I was habituated to walking long distances and on harsh terrains. When I reached home, I found Rakesh hadn't arrived yet. The sun had already set and night was fast approaching.

Rakesh, meanwhile, reached the gate of the sports ground. Not finding me there, he went in search of me.

He arrived home after a couple of hours. When he entered the house, he looked extremely worried and even in the modest chill of February, he had sweat running down his face. He looked scared and the first thing he asked when his mother opened the door was about my whereabouts. When he saw me come and stand beside his mother, he heaved a sigh of relief and told us that he was looking for me for the last three hours. He had been to each and every area in the city where I could have possibly gone. He said he had also asked my fellow sportsmen, but none of them had any idea about me. He told me that he would have gone to my village in Himachal Pradesh had he not found me at his home.

'If Chopra sahib got to know about it, he would have suspended me for leaving you alone like this,' Rakesh said.

I never thought that a small blunder could cause such a big confusion. How could he think that I had fled? I loved working there and in a short span of time, I had developed an attachment to the job, the people in my office and Rakesh's family, something which I had never experienced working anywhere before. I patted his back and apologized for leaving the ground without informing him.

Rakesh gave me my specially tailored tracksuit that I had to wear for any kind of sports activity. It was a navy blue suit with white stripes. I went inside, put on the suit, looked at the mirror and I loved it! The very next day, I was given a room in the hostel near the PAP ground. The room had a special bed, customized to my height. On one side of the room, there was a chair and a table and I was also provided with a small almirah. For the first time in my life, I got a furnished room of my own. I have no words to express how happy I was at that moment.

Fate seemed to have taken a sudden turn for me and in a span of less than six months, I went from a poor labourer to a bodyguard and now a policeman. It was an amazing feeling!

However, this was not the end of my good fortune. God was busy crafting a completely different story for me.

11

My Failures in Sports

I was happy with this new phase of my life and felt a childlike excitement within me.

Chopra believed that my height and build could help the Punjab Police earn accolades and respect in sports. 'I have very high hopes from you,' he would say to me.

I wanted to live up to his expectations. If he had not noticed and found me, I would never have got such an opportunity and respect in my life. Had he not been there to support me, I would have been stuck in the job of a bodyguard for the rest of my life. He had already helped me a lot and now it was my turn to repay him for his kindness.

When my training began, all I was told to do was run around the perimeter of the sports ground. Unlike present times, when the sports departments of the police have sophisticated sports equipment, we had none. Our training consisted of running for long hours. I used to get up and reach the ground before dawn and kept running the whole day around it. Every time an officer or a coach came to the ground, he would order me to run more and I used to follow this instruction without any objection. Many a time, I wondered if running continuously, day in, day out, made any sense, but of course, I couldn't say this aloud.

There was one person who used to sit in the stands and observe the other players practise when we had our training sessions. Time after time, he instructed and advised the players. He used to sit there watching us for long hours. I also noticed that all the other players revered him. They touched his feet and took his blessings. All this struck me as odd since I knew this man was not a coach but a normal policeman like us. Why should he then get to sit all day while we sweated it out on the field?

I decided to find out. Once, with the excuse of needing rest, I sat down beside the man and started a casual conversation. I asked him the reason for keeping away from the training. He replied that his knee was injured.

'And what is your salary?' I asked him.

'Rs 4000 per month,' he replied, taken aback a little by my sudden question.

I was shocked. I used to get only Rs 2800, which was obviously very little in comparison. Apart from this, I was told to run for four to five hours every day. At that time I couldn't help but feel jealous of this man. All he ever did was sit throughout the day and he earned almost twice my salary. I was furious and I made up my mind that I would not run from the next day.

The next morning, I got ready and came to the field and sat next to the man. Whenever anyone came and asked me why I was not practising, I said that I also had pain in my knee. Throughout the session, as more people came, I gave them the same excuse. Surprisingly, no one asked the other man any reason. Not a single person. This further fuelled my frustration. I thought that the man must be influential, which was why no one dared to ask him any question.

In the evening, I shared my thoughts with Rakesh, who told me that the man was not an ordinary person like me. He was a national-level basketball player. This was the reason he was greeted by everyone, instructed everyone on the field and held the senior post of an inspector of police. He also added that when I would do something significant, I would also be promoted in rank and would receive similar respect from everyone.

That night, I couldn't sleep. Rakesh's words reverberated in my ears. I needed that respect. I needed that position. I was not aware of the path, nor did I know what the journey would entail. All I knew was I would work harder and become an inspector. From the next day, I started running longer distances. My dreams got bigger and my determination got stronger, which lead to more rounds of running, stretching and sweating.

One day, while I was doing my usual rounds of practice on the field, Jarnail Sota, the shot-put coach, noticed me. He was a retired air force personnel, who had later been inducted as a coach in the Punjab Police. After observing my routine for a few days, he was clearly impressed. Later, he spoke to Chopra and selected me for his squad.

For the next few months, I played shot-put. Chopra used to take great interest in sports and in spite of his busy schedule, he used to visit the sports ground twice a day for the morning and evening sessions. He met almost every single player. He took great care of all the sportspersons, discussed their game and motivated them to perform better. He also ensured that everyone followed a good diet.

Desi ghee was considered a vital source of energy for a sportsman in those times. A meal without desi ghee was considered incomplete. The people not only consumed ghee in their cooked meals, but they drank it separately in bowls and glasses too. Being sportspersons, we were supposed to consume many cartons of desi ghee in a month. We were also given a kind of pickle that was non-vegetarian. It was considered a great source of energy. During those days, there weren't any external food supplements such as vitamin tablets, protein powders and other nutrients available, so we used to eat eggs, bananas, milk and desi ghee to supplement our diet and to build our stamina. In the present times, the market is flooded with energy supplements and the youth are taught to consume oil-free meals. They are also told to move away from natural things such as milk products and vegetables. Natural supplements and exercise are the best ways to both gain and lose weight. I still wonder why doctors suggest dieting and weight-loss products, instead of advising people to exercise.

Meanwhile, I continued practising for shot-put. Coach Jarnail Sota taught me many different techniques that would help me. He was a perfectionist and he ensured that we learnt even the smallest techniques that might get us better results. Right from holding the ball properly to placing it behind the neck above the shoulders to the delivery of the shot, he kept a strict eye on each and every movement.

My hard work and the coach's expertise seemed to bear fruit as I found my name in the list of candidates selected for the inter-state police shot-put competition. It was to be held in Jalandhar. It gave me immense pleasure when I saw my name on the list. For the first time, I understood the importance of my name. It further added to my confidence and I started devoting more hours to practice. I worked very hard, tried to learn all the tricks that the coach taught and practised at odd hours. I gave my blood and sweat in the preparation of the game. The motivation by Chopra was further encouraging and I felt happy at how my life was proceeding.

All the efforts, hard work and my strong determination paid off when I earned the first position in the competition. Though I was confident about my success, I had never imagined that I would end up defeating everyone. My shot was over 16 metres and no other shot was even close to it. This was my debut competition and my very first tryst with the sweet taste of success. I was ecstatic! It was a moment of pride and revelation.

There is nothing in this world more beautiful than the sense of achievement. When you feel good about yourself, when you feel proud of yourself, when you feel like your hard work has paid off, and when the result of all the sweat and toil spent during practice sessions is in front of you in the form of victory, the feeling is incomparable! The happiness to have attained the goal, which one had only dreamt about, is priceless. The sense of achievement is regardless of the nature of the success, the money earned or the level attained. Even the slightest form of success takes us away from our insecurities and self-doubts and makes us want to spread our wings and fly high.

Winning the shot-put competition was an achievement of this kind. I could hear my name being called over and over again. 'And the sportsman who has secured the first position in shot-put is Dalip Singh!' the announcer bellowed through the microphone. This was followed by a huge roar of applause from the crowd. The entire stadium reverberated with the sound of clapping. I saw my coach, the sports secretary and Chopra beaming.

I climbed on to the podium. I was delighted to receive the certificate and medal. The thundering applause did not seem to cease.

This victory instilled more confidence in me and I started practising rigorously. I doubled the number of practice hours and winning the national-level shot-put competition became my ultimate goal. I practised from morning till evening, oblivious to the unbearable heat of the sun. I reduced the number of meal breaks. I did not want to slacken even for a single moment.

Also, the expectations of people began to rise. I was now greeted in a different manner by everyone. The people in the PAP started to recognize me as a capable sportsman.

But then, life is a journey which comprises success and failures. At one point, you feel that you are lying on a bed of roses while in another moment, you find yourself surrounded by miseries. Things do not go as planned and sometimes there is an invincible barrier to success. I never realized that my plans to garner more fame and success would be interrupted by a severe injury. This came at the very juncture when my life was about to get better. One day while practising, I felt pain in my back whenever I threw a shot. A sudden, sharp pain would shoot through my back. The pain went on increasing and I had to stop my practice.

When the pain became unbearable, I was taken to a doctor. He examined my back and did a few tests. After examining me closely for the next few days, he told me to discontinue shot-put.

'How is that possible?' I asked. His words sounded unbelievable.

He told me that during practice, I had injured one of my muscles in the back and if I further risked playing the game, the condition of my spine might worsen. Therefore, I had to stop playing the game forever.

Playing shot-put had become my life and even the thought of chucking it was unbearable. In the past ten months, this game had given me everything I had dreamt of—fame, glory and respect—and now I had to give it all up. This was one of the most dreadful experiences of my life. I had dreamt of being a gold medallist in shot-put at the international level. Everything changed after this. My life came crashing down in the blink of an eye. The doctor informed me that my injury was due to the intensive and improper practice I had been doing on my own for a while. I was in shock for a few days. Meanwhile, all my fellow players, my coach and Chopra kept on motivating me. At that time, I realized how blessed I was to have these amazing people by my side. They truly had untainted souls. They made me believe how special I was and that God had sent me to this world for a special purpose.

Who says evil surpasses good in this world? I don't think so. The day that happens, this world would cease to exist. Just take the example of terrorists—they are only a handful, but on the other side, our army and police outnumber them tremendously. The only difference is that evil keeps on screaming about its presence and good remains silent. Good is the base this world is standing on.

It was a tough time for me. Leaving something that I cherished deeply, especially when I was mastering it and that too, as a result of something completely unexpected, was painful. It took me some time to overcome the trauma.

Meanwhile, I was told to try my hand at other games. I shifted to the game of discus throw.

I again challenged myself, but my back pain continued to trouble me and took me away from this game as well. I was then told to try horse riding. It turned out to be my third failure, as the horses were unable to run fast because of my weight and size. Finally, I got attracted to the game of boxing. I knew that I could be a successful boxer as it was a game in which my power could play a major role in my success. I was strong. I was fearless. And above all, I knew how to fight. But in the game of boxing, every morning, I was told to run. On inquiring about the reason, the coach said that it was the best warm-up exercise for a boxer. I continued to do so for another two months but I was not given a single chance to enter the ring.

My requests were turned down and I sensed that people were talking behind my back. Once, after asking the reason persistently, I was told that my power was tremendous and way higher than the other players because of which they wouldn't be comfortable boxing with me. I felt helpless as I did not have a counterargument. Yes, it was true that I was more powerful than the other players, but I never knew that this would work against me. As a result of being continuously neglected and never being given a chance to enter the ring, I quit boxing too.

Due to this sudden turmoil and shifting from one sport to another, I somehow began to lose my confidence. Despite my complete dedication and determination, I was not able to find that ideal sport where I could perform my best. However, deep inside in my heart, I knew that my hard work would pay off one day and I would be able to find a solution. Hence, I kept on motivating myself.

Meanwhile, my back pain lessened thanks to the timely medical aid provided by the doctors. Once, my doctor suggested that I should try bodybuilding. He said that with my body structure, I could do well in bodybuilding. It would not only strengthen my back muscles, but also improve my stamina as a sportsman.

I was really happy to have found such useful advice. However, when I went to obtain permission for it from Chopra, he had a different opinion. 'Bodybuilding isn't any sport,' he said. This was an unexpected response because from my very first day in Jalandhar, he was my constant support. I had always done whatever he had told me to do. I tried to play every sport that he wanted me to play. I didn't care for the blistering heat of the sun or the cold wintery mornings but kept on training relentlessly. I was extremely hurt. Then he suggested that I should try wrestling instead. I accepted it. However, according to the rules, a wrestler could not weigh over 125 kilograms. I was back to square one.

Where would this end? What was my destiny? I wondered.

12

Warm Up

One morning, I came to know about a bodybuilding competition which was scheduled to be held next month. All the members of the PAP sports department who had strong bodies were invited to participate in the competition. The organizers showed great interest in me and offered me an opportunity to join their gym after my practice hours at the PAP ground. Hence, without any second thoughts, I decided to give it a try.

On my first day at the gym, I was introduced to the other bodybuilders, some of whom were national-level champions. Soon, I started my hectic schedule. I used to complete my practice hours during the day and visit the gym in the evening. Such a schedule was tough to manage initially, but I got accustomed to it in a short span of time. However, I always felt that I needed to dedicate more time to bodybuilding if I had to win accolades in it. After persistent requests, Chopra permitted me to pursue bodybuilding full-time. He was moved by my keen interest.

My 100 per cent dedication yielded quick results. Chopra saw the changes in my body in a short period of time. I practised on a regular basis and was also taught the important techniques that I had to follow in order to build a good body. Our coach advised me to eat a protein-rich diet including eggs, potatoes and chicken. Also, I was advised to stop eating desi ghee as it was increasing the fat content in my body.

In order to build a perfect body, I needed to develop the muscles throughout my body including the neck, traps, shoulders, chest, biceps and calves. My schedule started with stretches, followed by hammer curls and leg curls. I began to do more extensive exercises with heavier weights. It was tough in the beginning. Though my body was used to hard work, this was absolutely different. I wasn't used to this regime of exercising. However, within a span of few days, I became accustomed to it. I began to develop and strengthen my muscles. Gradually, I learnt more and more exercises which were meant to develop and strengthen the other body parts. The best thing was that I found all this extremely interesting.

Excitement pulsed through my body when I held the dumb-bells. I observed that the other aspirants got tired after practising for a few hours while I never got tired. Perhaps, it was due to my deep interest or maybe it was because of the stamina God had gifted me with.

This routine continued for a couple of months till it was almost time for the bodybuilding competition. With the big day drawing closer, all the bodybuilders started devoting more hours to practice and also began taking better care of their diet. They increased their intake of fruits and eggs as well as protein-rich food such as chicken and fish. Emerging victorious in the competition seemed to be their only motive. There was a different vibe in the environment. The hope of coming out victorious was gleaming in every eye. I, too, thought only about victory. I hadn't forgotten the victory I had earned in the shot-put competition and wanted to feel the same exhilaration again, this time by winning the bodybuilding competition.

I was trained for striking different kinds of poses during the bodybuilding event. I was also given a bodybuilding suit, which was a one-piece suit that revealed my upper body. Initially, I was hesitant to wear it but this was a necessity. However, I felt extremely confident when the other people in the gym appreciated my body in the suit.

Just a day before the competition, I even made my hair look appealing and stylish. After all, the competition was all about showing off one's body and personality. I was confident that I would do well. I had built a good physique and had practised all the techniques taught by my coach. In addition to that, I had the advantage of my unusual height. But there was this slight nervousness as well. This was my first bodybuilding competition and I would have to go onstage and face hundreds of people, wearing a single-piece suit.

Finally, the day arrived. On my way to the venue, my coach reminded me of all the tips and tricks, and also told me to maintain physical and mental discipline during the competition. He told me to be optimistic throughout the competition. After this, he took me to the venue as the event was to begin in an hour. I did a final round of practice before entering the venue.

In the competition, I tried to perform to the best of my abilities and qualified for the top-ten round. I gave my best in the second round. However, I couldn't qualify for the third round. I was aghast. It was only after a while that I was able to calm down. Though I was disappointed at not being able to win, I was happy that I was selected amongst the top ten.

After just a few months of practice, being able to compete with professional bodybuilders and getting selected in the top ten was indeed an achievement.

Chopra was the chief guest in that competition and he was satisfied with my performance. After the show, lots of co-participants and visitors came and congratulated me.

When I returned to the PAP headquarters after the competition, I was warmly greeted by all the officials and other staff members. They treated me like a winner. Chopra was so happy with my performance that he promoted me. I was promoted from a constable to a head constable. Also, my salary was increased by Rs 400. From Rs 2800, it became Rs 3200. In addition to this, I was given a meal consisting of ten eggs, half a kilogram of milk and chicken every day. This was one of the most remarkable days of my life. I was extremely happy. Not only was I a policeman but also a professional bodybuilder. I had finally taken my first step on the way to becoming an inspector. I was finally a step closer to my goal.

Being in a positive environment helps you grow in life. One can devote oneself towards one's goal without any distraction. For me, the support I got from the PAP was a key factor which helped me to move towards my goal. When people appreciate you for your effort, it feels great. When people have to fight in spite of giving their 100 per cent effort because of issues such as dirty politics, they get bogged down and it leads to further deviation from a goal. For a sportsperson, positive emotions such as gratitude and appreciation are tools which help align his body and soul to strive for success and create history. Though in the later stages of my life, I had to face a lot of politics, I had by then reached a level in my career where setbacks did not affect me. At a very early age, I understood that I would have to be optimistic in all circumstances. I couldn't let go of any chance because of politics. For me, there was never a second chance. I will do it, even if I have to battle it out—that is what I believed in.

I continued to practise bodybuilding for another year without any trouble. Despite many challenges, I was finally happy with the way my life was treating me. However, at the gym, facilities were limited and both my fellow bodybuilders and I struggled a lot. The gym we used to practise in was not properly built. The building was old and dilapidated. The room was small and there wasn't enough equipment. But we were committed to our dreams and adamant about fulfilling them.

The roof of the gym was made of dilapidated tin sheets. The floor was made of mud. During the summer, the scorching sunlight made its way through those holes into the room and the blistering heat suffocated us. During the monsoon, the gym got flooded with muddy water as rainwater leaked through the holes in the roof. We then had to take our shoes off and keep them on a perch in order to protect them from getting wet. We then folded our trousers and kept practising. We were not ready to give up. I don't know why, but these hardships did not affect us. We were not bothered by them. In fact, it only made our determination stronger.

I want to share another fond memory from those times. I loved eating the chapattis prepared in the PAP mess. Many found them inedible but for me they were extremely delicious. Sometimes, my fellow sportsmen made fun of me when they observed me eating those chapattis with the excitement of a little boy but it hardly mattered to me. After hours of practice in the gym, anything tasted good.

Once, our coach informed us about the Mr Punjab competition that was to be held soon. He explained that this was a massive opportunity for all bodybuilders as it was a chance to get noticed on a larger and a far more glamorous platform. I made up my mind to participate in the competition. By then, I had built a very muscular body but I did not slacken my efforts. I pushed myself further. I put more hours into weightlifting and overall training as I wanted to win the competition at any cost.

The Mr Punjab competition was to be held at the Red Cross Bhawan in Jalandhar. There were participants from various cities as it was a big competition. This time, I qualified for all the rounds and entered into the finals. The top ten finalists had to present their well-built bodies onstage in front of the jury and the entire crowd. This is the time you have been looking for, I thought to myself as I waited for my turn to come. When my name was announced, I looked up at the sky, uttered a prayer and struck every pose I had been taught.

Ultimately, in the end, I was declared the winner. I was elated. It was a victory on such a big platform. I was ecstatic!

But this was just the beginning. Eventually, I won the Mr North India and Mr India competitions in the year 1997 and 1998, respectively.

With so many victories, I had now become a popular figure. My success story became a topic of discussion throughout the nation and I was interviewed by mediapersons from different states of the country. People were enthusiastic to know the reason behind my unusual height and body structure. Every person who I came across inquired about my diet. That was the time when there surfaced a large number of strange rumours. I even heard that 'Dalip Singh ate over twenty-five eggs at a single go!'

When people begin to talk about you and you get to hear new information about yourself every single day, it means that everyone is taking a keen interest in you and your affairs. In simple words, you are getting popular. This is the time when you can mould your fate. You need to control your emotions, ego and attitude so as to continue to welcome more fame and create more success stories. Had I been overconfident during that time or reacted negatively to the false gossip, I would never have got the opportunity to be the very first WWE wrestler from India or win the World Heavyweight Championship.

After I won the title of Mr India, I got a number of offers from different bodybuilding shows. I had to travel to different locations all around the country. In all these shows, I was required to guest pose (wherein a bodybuilder is invited to perform, but not compete). This not only gave me monetary benefits, but also provided me with an opportunity to interact with a large number of influential people.

I was now building my fan base in India. Whenever I went to guest pose in an event, I was always in the limelight. A common man from a small village of Himachal Pradesh had now become popular. However, I didn't feel much of a difference within myself. I was still the same. I loved to be among people and people loved me. Everything was going great.

Fame always brings money with it. For the first time in my life, I was earning thousands every month! I used to send the money home at regular intervals and the condition of my family also improved. I was happy that I was able to contribute significantly to their life. However, they still lived in the same small house. I now wanted to make a bigger contribution to their life by gifting them a bigger and better house.

We were a big family and therefore, I wanted to build a big house which could meet the requirements of all of us. For some time, the thoughts of building the ideal house kept me preoccupied. Whenever I went for any event and stayed in a hotel, I looked around to see how those spacious and comfortable rooms were constructed. After doing extensive research, I finally designed the entire plan for the house. I didn't hire any architect for this purpose. I single-handedly took on the project as I thought that no architect in the world could design the house of my dreams for my family.

This was a labour of love . . .

13

And the Real Fight Starts

November 1999

It is often said that good things come your way when you least expect them, and that God opens a door when you find darkness engulfing you. I lived an impoverished life, fought all the adversities that came with poverty and when I had given up all hope, God blessed me with a flick of his magic wand. My life improved all of a sudden. I now had a string of successes. I was not just provided with a comfortable life at the PAP, but I was also doing what I liked the most—sports and bodybuilding.

I did bodybuilding shows at different places as a guest performer. People appreciated me, my abilities and my body. I was comfortable with the money I received from these shows and the salary from the Punjab Police. Everything seemed to be falling on track. Life was progressing smoothly and for a person like me, who had always lived a life of scarcity, this was like a dream come true.

I was constantly thinking about how my life had panned out and what had been my motivation.

Being uneducated, I know the pain of not receiving a good education. I had to face a lot of hardships due to the lack of knowledge and communication skills. I remember feeling a sharp sting in my heart when people mocked me because I couldn't speak English, when I wasn't able to make quick calculations or when I wasn't able to fill the participation forms by myself for different bodybuilding competitions. I never wanted my brothers and sister to face the same situation. I made sure that they got a good education and a better lifestyle. At that time, the two most important priorities for me was to construct a house for my family in my native village and to provide a good education to my siblings.

A poor person can only aspire to think about how to earn food for himself and his family each day. A middle-class man, on the other hand, thinks of serving his family by getting a few comforts and a home. This is the maximum that a common man can aspire for. Above such aspirations lie impossible dreams, which most of us can't afford to fulfil. But despite being a common man, I dared to dream beyond the ordinary and was able to live my dream.

The start of a beautiful journey happened all of a sudden and unknowingly. I had not even heard of WWE, earlier known as WWF (World Wrestling Federation), which was an international professional wrestling competition at that time. Once, on a trip to Mangalore, I had a discussion with my friends and eventually, the discussion veered towards wrestling shows and WWE. That was when I heard of WWE for the first time. My co-passengers who were fellow bodybuilders informed me about a few of the popular WWE stars—The Undertaker, Kane, Big Show, The Rock and many more—who were popular all around the world. They were superstars and were loved by millions of people. I came to know more about their fight matches, their huge fan following and glamorous lifestyles. The life of these big stars fascinated me more and more and, throughout the journey, I kept on inquiring about them.

Some of my friends started comparing me with the best wrestlers of WWE. They made me believe that I could also be like those stars. They told me that if I were to go to the US, I could also be like one of them. I wasn't completely convinced by what they said but somewhere the conversations ignited my curiosity. Within the chaotic hustle and bustle of the train compartment, I began contemplating—can it be possible? Is there a place where all I have to do is wrestle and in return, I would get all the name and fame? I was so confident of my physique and strength that I believed I could defeat any wrestler in the world. A hope to live a life larger than my dreams and to have unimaginable fame and success began to take shape in my heart. As the train approached closer to its destination, I felt my life also moved towards a new destiny. But the journey to the goal is never smooth. It is racked by self-doubt and negative thoughts.

There are certain incidents in your life which boost your confidence and make you believe that you can achieve anything in life. But with the passage of time, because of our own doubts and insecurities, most of the aspirations die out. Our own doubts force us to think whether or not we are capable enough of achieving what we dreamt of. Hence, we defeat ourselves before life defeats us.

A similar dilemma gripped me. After residing blissfully in the land of dreams for a few hours, I suddenly wondered how

I would ever get to travel to the US. How could a person, who has never even travelled in the first-class compartment of a train, came from a humble background and couldn't even speak and understand English, ever get a chance to travel abroad?

So many doubts engulfed me. But the bug of success and fame had already bitten me. It had entered my mind and taken a permanent place there. I wanted to know more about the game, the players, the people and about how I could enter that competition. I had never seen any game of WWE but now I had an urge to watch them and learn.

When I came back to Punjab, I bought a battered second-hand black-and-white television set for Rs 1000 and got a cable connection installed. Then, I inquired about the timings of the WWE show from a friend and found out that it would be aired the very same evening. The problem was that at that very same time, I had to be in the PAP sports ground for practice. However, I was so eager to watch the show that I skipped my practice that day and rushed to my room.

And that was the starting point! As soon as I watched one game of WWE, a new dream was born. I wanted to be a part of it. It had everything I loved and the best part was the fame and success that came with it. It intensified my interest in wrestling and I found the moves fascinating. I was so moved that in the middle of the show, I got up and tried some of the moves in thin air.

This is my destiny—I told myself. I have always believed that God has made each one of us for a special purpose and that everyone has his or her own sets of strengths and weaknesses. There are a few who are able to recognize their abilities and use them to achieve their mission in life. At that very juncture, I realized that being one of the best wrestlers in the world was what I wanted to be. That was what could complete me. That was what I could do for the rest of my life.

I was well aware of the fact that there would be lots of problems in my path but battling challenges was my second nature now. That was what I had been doing since my birth—fighting with destiny. I was determined to face all the problems which would come my way in order to achieve my dream. Life had shown me the correct path and I was up for it, determined and passionate.

After I discussed the entire plan with my friends, I started to put together things for myself. I tried to look for sponsors who could send me to the US. I didn't have any idea of the requirements for going outside the country. I tried to know more and more about the required formalities. The quest began to find a suitable training academy, where I could get proper training to begin with and to practise the sport in a professional manner. My search ended at the All Pro Wrestling (APW) school in the US. Going abroad and enrolling in an academy needed a lot of money. Given my humble background, it was not possible. However, I had the good fortune to have supportive friends. They helped me with the financial issues and also with the formalities of applying to the academy.

I was all set to embark on a new journey but challenges have their way of finding me. It is often said that success is not well deserved if it is not preceded by its share of hurdles. I realized that I could not leave for the US without obtaining permission from the Punjab Police. This unnerved me.

I tried to get permission but I didn't get the approval. Without losing hope, I kept trying for two months. I talked about my passion, of how I believed that for the first time in my life I had found my true calling, and how badly I wanted to achieve it. The department's approval was the first key to my dream destination. But no amount of convincing on my part worked.

I wasn't ready to take no for an answer. Two weeks later, I again approached Chopra and requested him to grant me permission. He explained that he had confirmed from his resources that WWE was a dangerous competition as there were no rules and regulations for the safety of contestants. I was touched by Chopra's concern. It showed that he cared for me. However, I wasn't ready to give up on my dreams and was adamant to go there. Seeing my stubbornness, he told me to deposit my passport with the department. I had no other choice but to obey. I was disheartened but I knew that I would go to the US no matter what. I also understood the department's perspective but I have always been adamant about my goals of moving ahead.

A year passed but my dream of going to the US and fighting in WWE remained. I had no option but to curb my desires and wait for the right moment. Meanwhile, I practised bodybuilding and participated in a number of small-scale events. I got popular in the PAP as a bodybuilder. The sports staff appreciated me for my skills but this was not what I wanted. Though I resumed my normal routine, I always looked for an escape. And it finally came one day.

It was early 2000; I received the news about an Asia-level bodybuilding event which was to be held in Malaysia. Since it was a bodybuilding event, I desperately wanted to participate in it. The expense for participating in the event was Rs 40,000. The department refused to pay the expenses but returned my passport, saying that I could participate in the event if I wanted to, but I would have to manage the funds on my own. I didn't have that much money. Hence, even though I wasn't able to participate in the event, I managed to get my passport back. This was a golden opportunity for me and I began to plan my secret escapade to the US.

Putting my job at stake, I left for the US. Even though it was a risky choice, I didn't have any other alternative. I am a fighter and throughout my life I have maintained the spirit of a fighter. I have never been afraid of failure. I believe in execution. I never think too much. If I have to do something, I just do it. At that point of time, my life had become stable and I was doing well in my profession. I knew that every dream comes at its own cost and I was ready to pay that price. I chose to give up my stable life and ultimately, I went after my dream. I planned to stay with my friend who was settled in the US. He had his own home and lived there along with his family. I informed him about my arrival.

It was monsoon. I was born during the monsoon and my rebirth was going to happen during the same season. It felt like the right chords had been struck and the rains were a cosmic sign for me to forge ahead on my journey. So, finally, I packed my bags and got ready for a new country, the United States of America. To be honest, I was anxious and jittery as I was travelling thousands of kilometres to a country that was completely unknown to me, as was their culture, language and lifestyle. But I also knew that my determination was bigger than any hurdle in this world. I wanted to show the people in the US my power. I wanted to impress them. I wanted to make a mark right away.

After a long journey lasting almost a day, I finally arrived at the San Francisco airport. The academy had sent someone to receive me at the airport. I remember that while greeting him, I shook his hand with such force that he grimaced in pain. Idiotically, I wanted to show him how powerful I was!

The weather in the US was pleasant. It was unlike what I had left back in India. There wasn't any humidity or excessive heat.

I was initially taken to the academy where I met the owner, Rowland Zalander, and the coach, Dorobin Morgan. The academy was in a huge two-storeyed building, which consisted of a ring in the main practice hall with some equipment in one corner. In the centre of the front wall was a screen which displayed the fights of the wrestling champions. For the first time, I saw the wrestling ring which would become my *karmabhumi*, and so I touched it and bowed before it. Then, I was introduced to the students by the coach. My physique set me apart from the others. I saw people discussing my build and their expressions of surprise.

I was in a process of exploration—exploration of a new country, a new career and of my own self.

My journey had just begun!

14

Making of the Real Beast

For the first few days after I landed in the US, I stayed at my friend's place. Five days later, he told me that he could no longer accommodate me in his house and told me to find a place of my own. I could not say anything to him but I did feel bad about it. I thought of my days at Rakesh's home back when I had first moved to Punjab. I remembered fondly the love bestowed upon me by Rakesh's family and how they had treated me like one of their own. I smiled as I recollected his mother's selfless love for me. But here in the US, the situation was different. The people were different. Not having any other option, I silently picked up my bags and left the place. In an unknown country, lonely amongst an unknown crowd, I felt helpless and distressed. I didn't have any place to go and wandered about like a vagabond, I finally found an empty bench in a park and that is where I spent the night.

The next morning, I went to my wrestling academy and requested the authorities to arrange some kind of accommodation for me. There was no hostel facility available but keeping my distressed situation in mind, they allowed me to stay at the academy itself. I was provided a small room where they kept old and worn-out equipment. It was a storage room of sorts. There was also a small kitchen where I could cook for myself. I had to sleep on the hard concrete floor as there was no bed available. But all these hardships never bothered me as I had already survived worse situations.

Another big problem I faced was language. I knew no other language besides Hindi and a little bit of Punjabi. English was a language completely alien to me. I didn't know a single letter of the English alphabet. Trying to understand the meaning of sentences by listening to the conversations of others was an impossible task for me and I knew that it would not be easy. Initially, when the coach gave me lessons, I could not understand anything. However, I did not give up. Gradually, I started focusing on their expressions. I tried to follow their moves. Very soon, I got accustomed to it. I familiarized myself with some of the English words and learnt to study their body language.

Even though it was difficult to settle in at first, destiny was supporting me in different ways. By now, I had become friends with some of my fellow wrestlers, especially Corey. He was my best buddy and we used to roam around the city and watch movies in our free time. In those days, I was a big fan of Arnold Schwarzenegger and watched all his movies with great enthusiasm.

There was one interesting incident that occurred as a result of the language barrier. One day, I was sitting with Corey in a restaurant, happily munching sandwiches when I asked Corey to pass over the bottle of sauce.

'What?' he asked me.

'Sauce,' I said once again and pointed towards the ketchup bottle.

'What are you saying, man? This isn't sauce, this is ketchup,' he mocked me.

I didn't understand.

'What is the meaning of the word ketchup?' I asked him.

'Ketchup means "fuck you",' Corey told me.

Not having any idea of the words he taught me, I innocently believed him. After that incident, whenever he asked me 'What does ketchup mean?' I used to answer, 'Fuck you.' It was only later that I came to know that he was mocking me and all along I had been making a fool of myself.

With the passage of time, I tried to learn English as much as I could. From Dhirana to the US, it was hardly a time span of two years, but my life went through so many changes, and I left no stone unturned in order to adapt to the changing environments.

Apart from the rigorous training that I was a part of, I used to teach bodybuilding to students as I was a professional bodybuilder and in return, they offered me a ride to the gym, which was a little distance away from the academy. Hence, with time, I was well known amongst all the students in the academy.

My training sessions at the academy were gruelling. I always stuck to my schedule. My day started in the morning with cardio exercises, which should be done on an empty stomach. That was followed by breakfast at around 10 a.m. After this, I rested for some time. At noon, I would head to the gym to do three hours of exercise and weightlifting. After coming back from the gym, I prepared and ate my lunch, had it and rested. In the evening, there were regular practice sessions at the academy where we were taught different moves. For others, the day ended with this. But I discussed and learnt a few other moves from the trainers which I saw while watching WWE fights on TV. At night, when everybody left the academy, I practised on my own. When nobody was there to see me except that ring and the deaf and dumb walls, my screams reverberated around the hall. I came to the US with limited money and resources. So, I had to be successful. I was near the path of success but still it was away from me. I was worried as I did not want to go back to my place empty handed. Those sleepless nights, those injuries, those hours and hours of practice . . . perhaps, this was the making of a real beast.

Within a short period of six months, with all the hard work that I put in, I won the best student award at the academy. This opened the door of new opportunities for me. The academy started using me, my physique and my abilities in their advertisements. In a short span, I was already listed on the home page of their website.

However, everything does not go smoothly in life. Just when you think that you can control your life, it will surprise you in the most unexpected way. There will be incidents that will shatter you. These are the kind of incidents that happen all of a sudden, unknowingly, and will scar you forever. One such episode was the sudden demise of Brian Ong, a fellow wrestler at the institution, during a fight with me. I wish I could have saved him but it was not in my hands.

Brian Ong was a wrestler who was newly admitted to the academy. After the initial training for the first few days, he was to learn the spine burst—a complicated move, in which one of the wrestlers has to grab the opponent around the thighs or waist, lift him up, and toss him forward on to his back or slam him down while landing on top of him. It is usually performed against a charging opponent, using the opponent's own momentum to make the throw more impactful. In such a move, one has to ensure that he or she does not land on his or her head while falling. At that time, we were practising the same move and the coach was there to instruct us. I lifted Brian and slammed him down, but he wasn't able to move away his head from the ground and fell directly on it. Though it must have hurt him, he lifted himself up again at once. The coach scolded him and told him to do the same move once again in a proper manner. Out of rage and excitement, he removed his shirt and threw it outside the ring. We tried the same move for the second time, but he committed the same mistake again. His head hit the ground. He tried to get up, but failed and fell on the ground. His face turned white and he fainted. At once, the coach, the support staff and all of us rushed towards him.

Immediately, a call was made for an ambulance. We then took him out of the ring carefully and made him gulp down some water. In no time, the ambulance arrived and he was taken to the hospital. At that time, we had no idea that this accident would take a fatal turn. We thought he had got injured and would recover soon. I went upstairs and started preparing my food. I expected him to be back in some time. But my fate had something else in store for me. Within a few minutes, I heard the siren of police vehicles and the academy was surrounded by the police on all sides.

A few police officers came in and called me. They started asking questions which I had no answers to. I was not able to understand why I was being interrogated. I tried to ask my coach if Brian was all right but instead of giving me an answer, he told me to cooperate with the police. By now, I was a little worried as the situation seemed scary. I told them about my inability to understand and speak

English. They discussed something among themselves and made a phone call. After a few minutes, they made me talk to a person over the phone, who could speak and understand Hindi. He might have been a translator. I was asked a number of questions such as 'Did you take any drugs before the match?', 'Are you alcoholic?', 'Did you two have any clashes on some personal matter?', 'Did he take any drugs?' and 'What kind of relationship did the two of you have during training?' and so on. I was asked to describe the entire incident from beginning to end. I told them everything honestly as there was nothing to hide. They questioned me, and then cross-questioned me in between and I tried my best to answer each and every question calmly. At the end of the interrogation, I was instructed not to go out of the city and to stay in the academy till the police proceedings were over. I was still not told about the reason behind the investigation.

After the police officers left the academy, I asked the coach what was going on. It was then that he told me about Brian's death. My face turned white with shock. For a moment, words were stuck inside my throat. I didn't know what to say. I had never thought that a small accident would turn out to be that deadly. The agony and guilt that envelopes you on knowing that you have become the reason for someone's demise is unbearable. A person who was with us a few hours ago was no more and I was partly the reason for it. All of us were in shock. For the next few days, I was not able to concentrate on my game. Neither was I able to eat or sleep properly. I felt bad that this aspirational sportsman had to face such an end. Till today, that incident haunts me. It was one of the most painful moments of my life and one which I can never forget.

I was called by the police a couple of times for interrogation. After this, I was cleared from the case. I knew that I wasn't responsible for anything like this. I was completely shocked and shattered. It was tough to me to concentrate on the game again. I felt bad for his family. Later, his family won a lawsuit and was paid an amount of $1.3 million. But their loss could not be compensated by anything.

During those days, I felt that I had done something wrong. I was so distressed because of it that sometimes, I felt like leaving the sport forever and going back to my country. I was helped by my coach in APW who consistently motivated me to return to the ring. He tried to talk with me and helped me focus on the game again. It took a long time for me to come back to the game and focus on my goal.

Life is always unpredictable. You never know what is waiting for you at the next turn. Shortly after this, something happened which again strengthened my belief in God. I got the biggest opportunity of my life—a call from the World Championship Wrestling (WCW), one of the biggest platforms for a novice wrestler like me to showcase my talent. The selection committee of WCW expressed their interest in hiring me and offered me an opportunity which could open the gates of stardom and success in my life. I was exhilarated. I was near . . . so near that I could sense and feel it. The thought of being live on international television made me feel ecstatic. The name and fame I had dreamt of was about to come true.

I practised hard. My determination was stronger than before. But life was never too easy for me. Perhaps, my fate wanted me to wait and work more. When we were just about to get into the agreement, the WCW was sold to Vince

McMahon, the owner of the present-day WWE, which meant that my agreements were put on hold.

This was a big disappointment for me. For a moment, I felt that my dreams were shattered. That night, I didn't have my food. I didn't feel like practising. I moved out of the academy and roamed the streets of San Francisco. Though I tried to console myself, the raging anger against my own luck wasn't letting me do so. I had to prove myself and that too in a short time. I had a lot of liabilities and lots of expectations to fulfil. Another problem was that I didn't have enough money left with me to pay the academy fee for the next year. The incident with WCW made me insecure about my future. Here was an opportunity that I had waited for day and night and had given my life to, but when the opportunity came, it knocked on my door and left, leaving me depressed.

Such disappointments and hardships have taught me some important lessons. Life is all about overcoming such difficulties and embarking on a fresh start. There are times when life doesn't go the way we wish. You can't foresee every event of life. Failure and success are a part of it and they have to be accepted by everyone. Life could be unfair, but it is still a blessing. It is still a gift of God. I decided to move on. I had to explore the world and fulfil my dreams.

Hence, I strived harder. I continued to practise new moves, some of which I learnt by watching the WWE matches, while some were created out of my own imagination. I wasn't ready to give up; I was going to tide over every adversity.

15

The First Step

June 2001

I continued to practise. Somehow, the disappointment in the recent past increased my zeal to work harder. I began to practise more and more and increased my focus on improving the different moves. The loss made me realize that I had to put in extra effort. During those days, the desire to be successful was the only thing on my mind.

Soon I got another opportunity. This time it wasn't from the Americans, but from the Japanese. In the academy, we were told that a Japanese team would visit us soon. This team would be from the New Japan Pro Wrestling Company, one of the biggest and most popular wrestling companies in the world. It consisted of the world's best wrestlers and it would have been a great opportunity to get selected by them. Each of us was excited as this could be the turning point of our wrestling careers. Our days passed in huge anticipation. One day, the team finally arrived but we were disappointed. We had expected a team of men, all lavishly suited up, in expensive cars, but they came in a taxi and were ordinarily dressed. We had our doubts because in the world of wrestling, showing off means power. Did they really belong to such a big wrestling company like we had been told? We didn't say anything but our doubts persisted.

They visited our academy, checked all the trainees, made us show some of our moves and went back. We were still sceptical about them. But two weeks later, when we got the proposal from their side, our happiness knew no limits. They had selected three wrestlers amongst us and I was one of them. The best part was that the amount that was being offered to me was five times the amount offered to the other two wrestlers. So, finally, my journey in international wrestling began. It was for the first time that I had been selected by an international company and it was a moment of immense pride.

In order to visit Japan, I had to visit India first and get the Japanese visa. So, I came back to India, collected my visa and two days later, left for the much-anticipated Japan trip along with my fellow wrestlers. Our flight reached Tokyo, the capital city of Japan. It was one of the most beautiful cities I had ever seen. The weather was pleasant. There were a number of skyscrapers that were so high that they seemed to touch the skies. We reached there in the evening and as the sun gradually set and the night approached, the real beauty of the city came into view. By the time I reached my hotel, I felt at peace. This city seemed like the perfect place to start my new journey.

We reached our hotel at around 7.30 p.m. and after some time, we were taken for the city tour. The city had huge buildings. Some of these buildings were more than 150–200 metres high. We first went to the Tokyo Imperial Palace. It is a beautiful monument located on the site of the Edo Castle. It is situated inside a large park and is the residence of the imperial family of Japan.

The park was breathtaking. Besides a large plaza and the palace, there was also a beautiful bridge in the park, which was earlier a wooden bridge named Nijubashi. I enjoyed the time I spent there. We then went to the Edo Tokyo museum though I wasn't interested in the artefacts there. Also, by this time, I was feeling tired as I had flown a long distance and hadn't rested. After the tour, we went back to our hotel and had dinner. The very next day, we had to leave for the stadium where we were to be introduced to the crowd at 10 a.m.

Tring-tring . . . tring-tring. The buzz of the telephone disturbed my sleep all of a sudden.

I stretched my arms to pick up the receiver, grumbling under my breath. It seemed that I still wasn't over the tiring journey. I didn't feel like getting up from my bed and wanted to rest the entire day. I rarely felt this tired as I am always looking for an opportunity to utilize time in the best way possible. To put it in simple words, I never waste time. I am generally active and keep myself busy with something or the other. But it was different that day. It might have been the comfortable bed and the cosy room in that five-star hotel or it could have been the tiring journey coupled with the city tour.

Somehow, I stretched myself towards the phone and picked it up. The manager of the team was on the line. He was angry with me as it was already time to leave, and I was told to be ready within the next fifteen minutes. I was so tired and sleepy that I ignored him and fell back on my bed again. After some time, there was another ring on my phone and this time, I didn't even bother to pick up the call. I ignored the ringing of the phone but within minutes, there was a banging on the door.

Finally, I lifted myself up from my bed to open the door. I still felt lethargic and drowsy. When I opened the door, there were two people in front of me. One of them was my manager and the other person was a stranger. The manager screamed at me. It was fifteen minutes past 10 a.m. and he abused me for being late on the very first day. He was angry at my irresponsible behaviour. The entire bus was ready to leave and I had not even woken up. I did not retaliate as I knew the scolding was justified. I was the one at fault here. I apologized to him, got ready in a few minutes and left.

We reached the venue within half an hour. When I entered the wrestling courtyard for the first time, I looked around and saw a huge crowd. There were people in all the corners of the Tokyo Dome. Wherever I looked, there were people and they were cheering for us. When I entered the ring for the first time, there was a huge applause. For a moment, I was a bit scared and I looked in all the directions but I could hear nothing but the loud roar of the excited audience. Soon, the cheering made me more and more confident. When my name was announced—'The Giant Singh'—I lifted both my hands in the air and thanked the crowd. After this, the roar became louder and more powerful. I couldn't understand what they were saying but I knew that they were certainly happy to see me. The hard work of all these days seemed to have finally paid off.

After this, I had my very first fight. It was a tag team fight. A tag team fight is one in which there are two or more wrestlers in each team. I was tagged with Giant Silva, a wrestler known particularly for his height. When we stood in the ring, the crowd went mad. The average height of our tag team was seven foot and two-and-a-half inches, and the total weight was 805 pounds. It was my very first tag fight and our opponents were Yutaka Yoshie, Kenzo Suzuki, Hiroshi Tanahashi and Wataru. Defeating them wasn't a big deal for us. Neither did they perform the moves which we had mastered nor did they have well-built physiques like us. Though it was an easy victory, the intensity of the game was amazing. This was the very first time I had played on such a big platform and winning the first match felt great.

The rest of the day went in high spirits. I realized that I had found what I had always wished for, and had proved my talent in it. I was happy. In the evening, we were taken back to the hotel and a few minutes after I checked into my room, my manager came inside. I thought that he had come again to scold me but this time, he had a box with him. He came inside and without saying a word, opened the box and unveiled a blue sports watch.

'Make sure that you are on time from the next day,' he said to me and left the room.

Though he gave me the watch with a stern warning, I knew it was with the best intention. He did not want me to be careless. I felt a little humiliated because of my mistake and decided that it would be the first and the last time that I was late for any event.

A number of matches followed, one after the other. I won most of these, but I also lost a few. After every loss, I would watch the videos of those fights again and again in order to understand my weaknesses and master them.

It is extremely important for any person to know about his strengths and weaknesses. Generally, in our lives, we overlook our weakness to concentrate only on our strengths, which isn't the right thing to do. This is because one can never learn anything from his or her strengths as they will always be good at it, but one can learn from their weaknesses. A person will always attack another's weak points and mastering these truly makes one a champion in life.

I continued to work for the Japanese company for the next few months. During those days, I travelled frequently between India and Japan. I had to go to Japan only if there was an event; I stayed in India for the rest of the time.

16

The Love of My Life

January 2002

It is said that there are certain things, places or incidents that become so important to a person that they play a decisive role in one's life. For me, that special place would always be the PAP headquarters. It is the place which gave me my very first respectable job, its grounds were where I practised as a sportsman and it is the place where the desire to attain a life of fame and glory was born. Though the PAP authorities didn't support me in my dream of going to the US, they will always have a special place in my life. Even today, when I visit the headquarters, I feel like worshipping it like a holy shrine. The PAP has been a witness to the transformation of Dalip Singh Rana to The Great Khali. It has been a witness to my hard work, determination and willpower. When I got tired after practising for hours, the PAP grounds offered me its lap to rest. Its soil absorbed my sweat as its own.

When I came back to the PAP, I thought that Chopra would be angry with me as I had left without his permission.

I was scared to go to the PAP ground again. But I knew I had to face it anyhow. When I entered, Chopra gave me a stern look. It was difficult for me to judge what was going on inside his mind. I thought I would get a good scolding. But in the very next moment, he smiled. He came near to me and said, 'Proud of you, my son.' And then he hugged me. Perhaps, he would have understood what I was made for. Perhaps, he had stopped me previously because he was worried for me as I had never been anywhere outside India. Perhaps it was the concern of a mentor, a motivator and a guardian who wanted me to be successful but was worried that I would land into some trouble.

One of the most beautiful gifts that the PAP grounds gave me was the love of life, my wife, Harpinder Kaur. She has been a part and parcel of my success all these years. There was nothing extraordinary in the way we met; ours was a simple love story. I was in India at that time and it was during one of those beautiful, pleasant summer mornings that I saw her for the first time. I was on the PAP ground, resting after a round of cardio exercise, when I involuntarily spotted a girl not very far from where I was sitting. I had never seen her there before, so I guessed it was her first time on the grounds. She was dressed in the usual sports attire and seemed like a Punjabi to me. She was fair with long, lustrous, black hair that was tied into a braid. Her kohl-rimmed eyes seemed to be searching for something. When I saw her, there was a sudden enthusiasm to know more about her. I suddenly realized that I had been staring at her for over a minute now. I averted my eyes quickly. But moments later, I found myself gazing at her again. I had no idea why but I knew that I felt an instant attraction towards her. There was something about her nonchalant simplicity . . . something that was not letting me take my eyes off her. I had never felt something like this before. It was a sensation of nervousness and excitement at the same time. I couldn't decide what kind of feeling it was. All I knew was that I had this strange urge to talk to her. But I was not supposed to react in this manner as I was a sportsman and a policeman and that required me to be disciplined. Thereby, I buried my feelings and continued with my training.

The next day, I saw her again and felt my heart skip a beat. I kept looking at her on and off, and felt a strange kind of comfort when I saw her. Sometimes, I even saw her looking at me through the corner of her eyes. I didn't know what kind of feelings I was experiencing, but I knew it was something special.

That night, I kept thinking about her and it was strange, very strange indeed. I could not forget her face even for a second. I was so attracted by her that I found myself blushing while thinking about her smile. I never intended to lose my composure but this time, I felt as if I was going to lose myself to her. That night, there wasn't a single moment when I did not think about her. The next day, I had to leave for Japan. I went to the grounds in the morning, but she wasn't there. I inquired from a few other sportspersons about her but they also had no idea. So, finally, with no other option in hand, I left for Japan carrying the memory of her beautiful eyes and captivating smile in my mind.

Today, there are a number of social media platforms for young people, where boys and girls can connect and interact with one another. During those times, we did not have such luxury. The only modes of communication then were letters and landline phones. Even cell phones were a rare luxury. For me, the only way to preserve my feelings for her was to keep her image in my heart. At that time I didn't know that

I was in love with her. I kept thinking about her for long hours. It was tough for me to concentrate on the fights, the matches or on other things. For the first time, the thought of an unknown girl seemed to overpower everything else. I wished to go back to India to catch a glimpse of her. I wanted to meet her desperately. Hence, I came back to India earlier than my scheduled day.

I was back in India and the first thing I did after I reached the city was to go to the PAP ground. I reached the ground and asked one of my fellow sportspersons about her. I was relieved when I got to know that she would come in the evening. For the entire day, I kept thinking about how to introduce myself to her and what to say to her. I was a little nervous and there were a number of questions which created doubts in my mind. Throughout the day, I kept thinking about how I would approach her.

Finally, in the evening, when I was in the canteen, I saw her coming towards me. My heart started thumping hard against my chest. All of a sudden, I started feeling uneasy. I was sweating profusely and my heartbeat accelerated. She came and sat at one of the tables near me. She was all alone and looked at me once. For a moment, my heart skipped a beat. Should I go and talk to her? I asked myself. But what if she takes it in a wrong way? My mind argued. She won't kill you. Go and talk to her like a gentleman. My heart tried to motivate me. In the battle of my mind and heart, finally my heart stood victorious and I decided to approach her.

I went up to her. 'Can I talk to you?' I asked gently.

She gave me a surprised expression and didn't utter a word.

'I am Dalip,' I could barely speak.

'So?' she snapped.

'Actually, I . . . I want to talk to you if you don't mind,' I stammered.

'Okay,' she replied.

For the next few seconds, we kept looking at each another. There was an awkward silence between us. Finally, I broke the silence and said, 'I am from Himachal and you?' I made a desperate attempt to strike a conversation. She looked down. She was blushing. Not knowing what to say next, I told her that if she wasn't comfortable, then I would leave.

'I am from Jalandhar. My father works for the Punjab Police and we live in the PAP residential quarters.' Finally, she lifted her face and replied, a lot gentler this time.

We kept talking for the next two hours. Six cups of tea and three plates of assorted pakoras later, we were still talking. We still felt hungry—hungry for each other's company. Sometimes, only a few minutes are enough to understand each other and sometimes even one whole lifetime is not enough. But in our case, luckily, the former was true.

From that day onwards, we met on a regular basis. I was exploring this new aspect in life for the first time and loved it. We used to meet in the evenings, at the same time and same place every day. She told me about her family, her dreams and her aspirations and I became her patient listener. Her father worked as a head constable in the Punjab Police. They were four siblings and she was the eldest.

You would be surprised to know that we never met outside our sports ground. We never went to a restaurant for a romantic candlelight dinner nor did we ever go out for a movie. We were simple people, so were our lives and aspirations. We were more than happy with our chai–pakoras and long conversations. Sometimes, words are not required to describe feelings because eyes express everything. We were well aware of each other's feelings and we both knew what we wanted. We understood each other quite well. I suppose that a great sense of understanding is the primary key to sustain any relationship.

Our relationship grew stronger within no time. The best part was that she had no problem with my passion for wrestling. She had a positive attitude and was considerate. She did not mind my hectic schedules when I had to go abroad frequently.

Finally, one fine day, during our usual evening rendezvous in the canteen, I mustered up the courage to ask her the most important question, 'Will you marry me?'

She smiled, blushed and hid her face in her hands. We forgot about the tea. It lay there untouched, getting cold. For a few minutes, she didn't say anything. Both of us kept looking at each other, completely speechless. Then, all of a sudden she began to laugh loudly. I was confused. I didn't know how to react until she uttered—'Yes'. The very word my ears were yearning to hear.

My happiness knew no bounds. I was on cloud nine. I didn't know what to say next. I was absolutely speechless. Her acceptance was like a remedy for all my woes and difficulties. I felt as if I had achieved a new goal in life. I now had somebody to support me for my whole life. I had someone with whom I could share my desires, ambition, successes and failures. My life had moved on to an important phase in my life, and this marked the new beginning.

Harpinder and I shared a special bond of understanding. We discussed everything related to my work and my dreams. This was important as it was my passion in life. For years, I had dreamt of being a wrestler and she knew it well. I told her about the difficulties she might have to confront. I also told her about the uncertainties associated with my career. I wanted to make her aware of the risks involved so that we shouldn't have any problems later in life. Also, I told her how her support would be essential for me to achieve my goals and asked her if she was comfortable taking on such a responsibility.

I was happy that she was positive about everything. Perhaps, she was among those rare souls whom God had sent specially for a person like me and perhaps, falling in love with her was destined.

However, life was not a bed of roses for us. The real hurdle was yet to be crossed. I was a Rajput while she belonged to a Punjabi family. There was a huge difference between our cultures, rituals, family status and lifestyle. Though I knew that I could manage to convince my family to accept this inter-caste marriage, we were not sure about how her parents would react when they got to know about us.

She promised to talk to her parents that evening about us and our decision to get married. I had to leave for Japan the next day. We talked for a while and then left the PAP canteen. All I could think of was about her parents' reaction to our plans. It was important to me because our futures rested on their decision. I reached my room and tried to calm my nerves and sleep. But I wasn't able to sleep even for a second. I got up and paced up and down the room in anticipation. In those days, there were no cell phones, so the only option was to wait for the next day. For the first time since I joined the PAP, I missed the evening workout at the gym. To be honest, I was extremely worried. What if her parents didn't accept me? The negative thoughts haunted my mind. I tried to sleep again but failed, and kept tossing and turning till daybreak.

Next day, with the heavy weight of the unanswered question on my mind, I left for Japan. I was carrying an additional burden on my journey, the burden of the uncertainty of my relationship. As soon as I landed in Japan, the first thing I did was to call her on her landline number. I could feel my heart pounding as the call connected. Finally, I heard her voice.

'What happened? What did they say?' I asked.

'They wish to meet you in person,' she replied. 'Only then will they take a decision.'

This was a relief for me. At least, they had not rejected me straightaway. We still had a chance. That short stint (of about ten days) in Japan was the most restless period in my entire life. I wanted to fly back to India as early as possible. I wanted to meet her parents and talk to them. I wanted to convince them of my love for Harpinder. I wanted to make them understand that I was serious about my decision and would dedicate myself wholeheartedly to the relationship. Oscillating between excitement and nervousness, I somehow completed my stay in Japan and came back to India.

I had to meet her family the very next day and for the first time in my life, I dressed up in a formal outfit—black trousers, off-white shirt and a pair of brand new leather shoes which I had bought from the US. I combed my hair and applied a gel. I tried to look as decent and presentable as possible. When I was done, I made sure that I took a second opinion on my looks from my friends. After all, I was going to face my biggest fight that day—the fight for my love. I wanted to impress her parents at any cost.

Finally, I reached Harpinder's home. I met her family. They seemed like nice and friendly people. Matters unfolded in a lot easier manner than what I had assumed. I was asked about my education, income, profession, future plans and so on. I tried my level best to convince them and assured them that I was the perfect match for their girl. When asked about the wedding date, I told them that I would be going to Japan the very next week. All rituals could be done only after my return. However, they insisted that the *shagun* (the pre-wedding ritual) should take place before I leave for Japan as it marks the formal acknowledgement of the relationship between the bride and the groom's family.

Initially, I refused and told them to wait till I came back from Japan, but they wanted it to be held before I left the country. So, within a couple of days, the ceremony was organized. When I called and informed my parents about it, they didn't believe it and thought I was joking. It took a while to convince them. Further, to my surprise, when I told them to come to Jalandhar, they refused because they were doubtful why anyone would be willing to get their daughter married to someone who had a huge physique like me. They told me to get married first and then come to the village. So, from my family, only my younger brother and some of my friends attended the ceremony. From the girl's side, all her relatives and friends were invited. It was a small function and everything went smoothly. I felt happy and victorious. There was suddenly a new inspiration to lead my life well.

After a few days, I left for Japan but this time, I didn't carry the weight of anxiety with me. In fact, I felt satisfied and happy. The burden of uncertainty which was troubling me during the last visit had vanished completely. This time, Harpinder was mine, for my entire life, and I could plan my future with her. I knew that with her in my life, things would be quite easy. I believed that I would be able to deal with hardships and get the strength to face any adversity. I was assured that with her in my life, I would achieve new heights in my career.

I was in constant touch with her during my trip to Japan. Every day, we would talk on the phone, though only for a few minutes. What started as a conversation between two shy people had developed into a beautiful love story that only became stronger with each passing day. I could feel how much she loved and cared for me every time I spoke to her.

It was tough to find an accurate date for our wedding because of my busy schedule. Harpinder's parents were getting impatient and wanted to get it done as early as possible. So somehow, I managed to take leave for a week for my wedding.

My wedding was held on 27 February 2002. The initial ceremony took place in Gurudwara Jandiala Sahib in Jalandhar and after that, we headed off to my village for the remaining ceremonies and the wedding reception.

The reception dinner was a huge affair and people from nearly twelve villages were invited. There was fun, food and frolic for the next three days as people sang and danced to congratulate the newlyweds. As for the both of us, it was one of the most memorable days of our lives. Our love was finally culminating into togetherness for life. We could not have been happier.

17

An Unseen World

I have heard that life is a race. As far as my own life is concerned, I have been running from one end to the other since my childhood. At one time, it was for my daily bread and butter, then for my dreams and now for the people who love me. I always have this desire to do something for them. I don't want this journey, this race, to find an end. I have enjoyed every bit of it. However, as I have always said, every dream comes at a cost. In order to achieve our dreams, we need to work hard. We often come across certain situations in our lives that are unavoidable. Sometimes, we have to fight our own desires. It is in these situations that we have to compromise our personal interests and choose our professional liabilities. Being a wrestler, I had to face some such moments, where my mind had to go through indecisiveness and confusion, and I finally had to make some tough choices.

A week after my marriage, I had to leave for the US to sign some legal papers for my agent. As a result, Harpinder and I didn't get much time to spend with each other. I knew that at that time I should have been with her but in the choice between professional duties and personal desires, it's always the former which wins. I had signed a contract with the Japanese company and had to obey their orders. There was no other way out. Hence, with a heavy heart, I went to the US.

I checked into my hotel. From the reception counter, I got to know that the international calling facility was available in the rooms. Hence, the first thing I did after checking into the room was to make a call to Harpinder. We talked for about an hour and at that time I wished I could have brought her to the US with me. During the day, I got busy in other professional activities but after dinner, I rang her again and this time also we talked for about one hour.

The next morning, someone knocked on my door. It was one of the hotel staff and he had come with a telephone bill of $1860! I was shocked beyond words. I stared at the paper with wide eyes. Though I had talked to her for two hours, I had not realized that it would cost me so much. I felt there was something wrong. I was filled with rage and walked up to the hotel manager. Such a huge bill made no sense. Initially, he was adamant that I had to pay the entire bill. But after a heated argument, the manager checked the system and found that there was some flaw in their calculation. Finally, I paid the revised bill of $520.

I realized he was trying to cheat me. Had I not argued, I might have had to pay the entire amount.

Meanwhile, I continued to work with several other Japanese wrestling companies up until 2004. Though I was in a profession of my choice, I had still not reached my final destination. I had dreamt of bigger horizons. In between my hectic schedule, I once came to India on a casual visit. I was on my motorcycle and was heading towards a nearby village to fetch milk when I got a call from my agent in the US. He told me that a big production house wanted to sign me for a movie. Like any other person, I too used to take a keen interest in the movies and the breathtaking action scenes, especially of Hollywood movies, always appealed to me. I was fascinated by the beautiful locations and the kind of life depicted in these movies. This was an opportunity I had never thought of even in my wildest dreams. My first question to him was, 'Are you serious?' The next one was 'Will I be getting paid for this?'

Well, at that moment, I had no idea how big an opportunity this was for me. I didn't even know what I would have to do in the movie. I just packed my bags and two days later, left for the US.

My audition was held in Los Angeles where I met the movie's director, Peter Segal, and the Hollywood superstar Adam Sandler. The moment Sandler saw me for the first time, he said, 'This is what I need. Amazing! I want this man in the movie.' I was selected for the role and soon signed a contract with the production company. The title of the movie was *The Longest Yard*. Later on, I came to know that The Big Show and Giant Silva, famous wrestlers of WWE, had also been approached for the same role but it was I who got the opportunity in the end.

I had no idea about the world of movies. The first thing that I had to learn for the movie was to play American football. I also had to be taught everything related to acting. I was taught the moves and acts which I had to perform for the movie. I was trained to speak my dialogues with an English accent. Everything was taught in a simple manner, so that I could understand the lessons well. Also, it was ensured that I got enough time for my practice to build my fitness.

It was a long shooting schedule of around six months. Half of the shooting was done in Mexico and the latter half was shot in Los Angeles. I had the time of my life while working for *The Longest Yard*. I was awestruck by the luxurious lifestyle of Hollywood stars. Prior to that, I had never imagined that there could be a life so grand—stylish suits, posh apartments, seven-star hotels, expensive cars, late night parties and much more. Everything was so classy. The luxury was evident in the process of movie making as well. Every movie set was designed in such a way that it seemed beyond amazing. It seemed like I had come to heaven. Everything was beyond my imagination. I was provided a limo along with a chauffeur to travel anywhere in the city and whenever I went outside, a beautiful girl was always there to escort me with an umbrella. Even the crew members were friendly and always eager to help. I was provided everything that I desired and life could not have been grander.

One such incident reminds me of the warm relations I shared with my co-stars. Once, after I had shared the pool with one of the female models, Sandler and the other crew members teased me about it. Whenever they did so, I just reacted with a friendly smile. Fun and frolic was at its peak during that period. The presence of Sandler made the environment warmer. He was friendly with me and in no time, we became good friends. During the shoot, I also befriended Nelly, a world-famous singer.

The movie was released in May 2005 and was an instant success. It was appreciated by people from all over the world and my role was liked by a number of people. I received visibility on an international level. I was now in the hearts of millions of people. More people began to recognize me. This movie opened the gateway for appreciation from all over the world.

The Longest Yard somehow helped boost my career. It was when I came for the movie's promotion to New York that I got a call from WWE saying that Vince McMahon, the CEO of the company, wanted to see me. I could not ignore such an offer and accepted it instantly. After all, I had been waiting desperately for this call for years. On the scheduled day, they came to pick me up in a limo. It felt great. The venue of the meeting was half an hour away from my place. There I met McMahon and Johnny Ace, the director of talent relations at WWE. When they saw me, I could sense that they were impressed. After that, I was told to go inside the ring and show some wrestling moves. Without any hesitation, I did it. While coming back from their office, I knew I had hit the bull's eye. I was not wrong and within a few days, I got an offer from WWE.

I was close to my dream—a desire that had crept into my heart after seeing a WWE match on TV years ago in my hostel room in Punjab was finally getting fulfilled. What had seemed like an impossible dream back then was finally happening. Success seemed closer than ever before.

18

Opening My Own Gym

September 2005

Right from the days of poverty to the heights of success, my family has always been of utmost importance. My mother, father, brothers and sister, and now my wife—all have the most special place in my heart. Even as I reached new heights of success, I made sure that I never forgot my roots, my home and my village. So, every time I had some time on my hand, I would visit my homeland, even if it was for a few days. This time, I had a special reason to visit my village; it was my wife Harpinder. It had been long since I had seen her. At that time, there was no video chat facility through which we could see each other. We both longed to meet each other. It had been quite a long time since we had seen each other. Hence, I left for India as soon as I got a break from my hectic schedule in the US.

During my stay in India, a few mediapersons approached me with the request for an interview. I readily agreed to it. Amongst various things, they requested me to shoot the entire interview in a gym as they thought it would be a more appropriate location, given my personality and profession. Since I was a regular member of a gym in Jalandhar, I decided to get it done there. So we scheduled the interview for the next morning and planned to meet there at 9 a.m.

I reached the gym at the scheduled time and saw that they were already there. They were preparing for the shoot and were adjusting their cameras and other devices. After setting up everything, they politely requested the people who were working at the gym to move out of the range of the shot for a few minutes. It was a small request and there was nothing to be offended about.

Many of the people were co-operative; they readily agreed and moved away without asking any questions, but some of them took this in the wrong sense and refused to move. Even after repeated requests from the media team, these people did not budge. I decided to intervene. I assumed that since I was a fellow member of the gym, they would listen to me but that did not happen. They were hell-bent on creating a scene. I tried my best to pacify them but to no avail. Instead, they made a phone call to the gym owner and complained about it. The gym owner reached there within ten minutes and as soon as he saw the mediapersons along with their cameras, he lost his temper. Absolutely out of control, he began to hurl the choicest of abuses at them. When I tried to talk to him, he accused me of using his private property without any prior permission. He didn't even care about the cordial relation we shared. I again tried to persuade him to listen to me and tried to make him understand that our intention was not to disturb anyone. However, he was not in a mood to reason with us and was stubborn about us leaving the premises.

This made me realize that in life, we meet different kinds of people. Some become a part of our happiest memories, while others hurt us with their behaviour. Sometimes, the people from the latter category instigate us to prove ourselves. Quite ironically, they motivate us to identify our strengths which we didn't know existed with us.

The thing which bothered me the most about the incident was not the refusal but the rudeness with which it had been conveyed. His misbehaviour with the mediapersons bothered me because they were there because of me. Finally, when nothing seemed to work, they left the place. I apologized to them for the inconvenience caused as I really felt bad for them. I wasn't bothered only because an interview had been cancelled that day, but because it was an attack on my self-respect. Throughout the day, I couldn't erase that incident from my mind nor was I able to sleep that night. I kept thinking about it again and again. I was agitated and anguished and didn't want to go to that gym ever again. While I was lying in bed that night, an idea struck my mind.

Why don't I open a gym of my own in Jalandhar?

Before the dawn broke, a decision was made. I needed my own gym at any cost, no matter what I had to do for it. From the next morning, I began to work on the idea. Soon, after considering a lot of options, I bought a piece of land and started the process of construction. However, nothing in life is quite as easy as it seems to be. It is easy to dream but achieving it is a different task altogether. I thought that for a person like me, it would be quite easy to construct a gym. However, I had never imagined that I would be short of funds. I got worried. At that point of time, it was my wife, Harpinder, who stood right next to me as my pillar of strength. She offered me her jewellery and told me to sell it and manage the funds. She thus made one more sacrifice, silently, without any complaints. I was hesitant but she persuaded me to do it.

Finally, the day came when I stood in my own gym with the same mediapersons, shooting the same interview that we weren't able to take earlier. I opened a gym at Rama Mandi, Jalandhar and named it Rana Health Club. It had all the modern facilities and equipment. Jalandhar is north India's biggest sports equipment market, so I found no difficulty in arranging all the required machines and other equipment. It was because of my wife that I was able to fulfil this desire to set up my own gym. That moment, I felt that all the pain that we had gone through had been worth it.

19

A Difficult Coach

I spent a fortnight in India. During those days, I spent a lot of time at my gym. As I had already become a popular face in bodybuilding, we got an exceptional response. There was an unprecedented number of enrolments, which increased day by day. I wanted to ensure that it was properly managed even in my absence. I employed skilled trainers and a manager, who could take care of the gym and the activities in it. After this, I went back to the US.

But this time, I wasn't alone. My wife was also with me. With the consent of my family, I had decided to take her to the US. For the first time in the last few years, I didn't board the flight alone. I had someone to talk to during my journey. It is a beautiful feeling when your soulmate is with you when the most beautiful chapter of your life is about to begin.

We landed in the city of Atlanta, where my training was scheduled. We were provided a beautiful and spacious apartment to stay. It had all been arranged by the WWE. It was also beautifully located on the edge of the city. There were all kinds of facilities and comforts. The training team had been especially directed to provide me complete training in the best manner possible.

Little did I know that things would not turn out to be as easy as I had thought at that time. My experience with my first coach turned out to be nothing short of a nightmare. He was a rude and frightening man. All the trainees used to be scared of him. He was an extremely dominating person and liked to do things his way.

I have seen that in the game of wrestling, there are players of different kinds. Every wrestler has his or her own strengths and weaknesses and they have to be trained accordingly. Some of them have a normal body structure, so they have to work on their movements, technical abilities, jumps and athletics to become good fighters. Others possess a huge body structure and rely on their strength and use throws, locks, takedowns, pins, gripping and so on to sustain a fight. Therefore, I feel it was important for the coach to vary the routine for each one of us.

I belonged to the latter category that relied on physical strength. I was not born to be a gymnast. I was a professional bodybuilder. My body and my physique were my assets. I wanted my instructor and coach to understand this, but he wasn't ready to listen to me at all. Initially, I requested him to assist me in the exercises and the warm-up, but he refused and ordered me to run. I obeyed his orders. I wanted to believe that he was trying to do what was best for me. And hence I tried to cooperate with him in every possible way.

However, later on, I discovered that that was not the case. According to him, we were supposed to follow his training methods without asking any questions. He would order me to run long distances daily. It was senseless and it had a negative effect on my body. Plus I was not comfortable with it. I repeatedly tried to explain to him and make him understand, but when nothing seemed to work out, I stopped listening to him. I started doing my workouts on my own without any support and tried to follow the moves I had learnt from the video recordings of the previous WWE matches. When the coach saw that I was doing my training according to my will, he began to get more difficult. After a few days, the environment became more and more hostile and it was getting impossible for me to follow my routine training.

Though I did try my best to control myself, I burst out finally one day. I had a heated argument with my coach.

As expected, he did not take my retaliation lightly. He stopped all the services that were provided for me. Even the help I used to get from my fellow trainees and other support staff was discontinued.

One evening, my wife asked me to take her to the grocery store to refill some of the groceries. I called my company office and asked the officials to send somebody who could drive us to the grocery shop. To my shock, I was told that nobody was available. Never before in the last few months had this kind of response been given by them. I knew the reason behind it.

I was helpless. I had never moved out of my apartment in the US on my own. Neither did I know the way to the grocery store nor did I have the contact details of any local cab company. I boiled with rage inside. How could a person be so mean as to not understand the problems of others?

I told my wife about my plight. I apologized to her because I was the reason she had to face these problems.

Again, she backed me and stood by my side. She told me not to worry and to look for solutions instead. We then decided to go off on our own to get the groceries.

We inquired from a few people about the route to Walmart but all we were able to understand was that it was at some distance from our apartment. We came to the roadside and tried to find a taxi but weren't able to find any. We kept walking in the direction people guided us to but after some time, Harpinder felt tired. We sat on the footpath to catch our breath and rest for some time. I looked around to see if a cab could drop us to Walmart and while I looked here and there, a car stopped in front of me. I wondered if somebody from the company had come to fetch us. In a few seconds, I saw a couple step out of the car and walk towards us. They seemed amazed to see me.

'Hey, I believe you are the same person who acted in *The Longest Yard*?' the man asked.

'Yes, I am Dalip Singh,' I replied.

'Oh . . . Wow!' All of a sudden, there was a big smile on his face. He said that he had always wished to meet me. He added that he was amazed at my body structure and wanted to know the reason for it.

We talked for a few minutes. Then, he requested me to sign an autograph for him and his girlfriend and also asked me if they could click a photograph with me. I readily agreed. Then, he asked whether we were stranded and needed some help. I told him that we had to go to Walmart. I also added that we had misunderstood the directions and were confused about where to go.

To this, he warmly offered to help. Initially, I felt a bit hesitant about taking help from a stranger but when he insisted again and again, I agreed. Not only did they take us to Walmart and help us in shopping, they even drove us back to our apartment. He also gave me his number and asked us to call him any time we needed help. For us, he was like a messenger of God and after this incident, he often came to visit us. He was not a mere fan now; he was a good friend. I still have fond memories of him when I look back to the chapters of my life in the US.

Meanwhile, the behaviour of the coach didn't change at all. It was like a cold war was being fought between us. Neither did I speak to him nor did I take his support for my training. He didn't miss any chance to create problems for me either. I soon discovered that I wasn't the only victim of his ruthlessness. Many other wrestlers were having a tough time too. So finally, when nothing seemed to work out, I complained about his behaviour to the director of talent relations.

He was a professional person and used to give high regard to the needs of the wrestlers. He ensured that nothing went wrong, whatever be the case, and respected the wrestlers. My complaint was taken seriously and a secret investigation was carried out. He asked the other trainees about the coach's behaviour and observed the proceedings quite closely for the next few days. One day, he spotted the coach shouting without any reason at one of the trainees. He was told to come to Johnny's office immediately. The coach's face was a little pale by now and the furiousness which he used to display had vanished. Within a few hours, the news of him being fired was all over the training centre of the WWE in Atlanta. This came as a huge relief to many of us.

After some days, I saw him at the gym where I used to go for my daily workouts and he looked like a changed person. He greeted me and tried to strike up a conversation. When

I asked him why the company fired him, he began to cry. He was still not ready to admit his mistakes and believed that somebody had conspired against him. He also tried to convince me that he never had any kind of grudge against me and that I had always misunderstood him. Though I said nothing to him, there was only one thought that preoccupied my mind while listening to him—'As you sow, so shall you reap.' Often in their lives, people feel that they can mistreat others and get away with it, but this is not true. God is there to observe the actions of every individual. If you inflict pain on someone, your karma will get back to you. We should never forget that life is like a boomerang; what you do to others will surely come back to you one day.

20

The Launch—A Surprise for the World

April 2006

My formal training was over by now and I was all set and fully prepared to get into the ring. There were a series of discussions over my launch in the WWE. The entire WWE management, including McMahon, wanted me to be introduced to the world in a grand way. They wanted my launch to leave an unforgettable impression on the world. In simple words, my launch had to make a statement. For months, the WWE had kept my selection a secret as they didn't want the world to know about me beforehand. A seven-foot-two-inch tall giant from India would definitely have made news. Even the backstage and the frontstage teams didn't know about my launch.

The big day finally arrived. The match was going to be held between two stars of the WWE. On one end was The Undertaker, the ultimate champion of the game, while on the other side was Mark Henry, the world's strongest man.

During that time, the name 'The Undertaker' was synonymous with the word 'fear' and he was the living legend of the game. He was called the 'Man of Mystery' and his presence in the ring made the audience go crazy. He was given the highest regard and everyone respected him as the godfather of the WWE. Fighting against The Undertaker was a matter of pride for everyone. The entry sequence of The Undertaker in the WWE matches was in a manner different from the other wrestlers and it instilled unshakeable fear in the opponents. When he entered the stadium, there was a strange kind of stillness in the air. As he walked towards the ring, one could see the growing fear in the eyes of the opponent.

The two wrestlers were going to fight in a Smack Down match. Smack Down is a WWE tournament which started in the year 1999 and had become one of the most popular tournaments run by them. In the game contested in 2006, Mark Henry entered the ring and The Undertaker entered in his own style, spreading fear everywhere. As he entered the ring and removed his round hat, the crowd gave a huge roar. After this, he closed his eyes and faced the crowd. And then all of a sudden, he was attacked by Mark Henry from behind. But he was able to duck his head. After this, he began to prove his might. He punched Mark Henry in his face and didn't stop. He kept hitting him before he could retaliate. After that, he forced him to move to the other corner of the ring and rushed head first into him. This time, Mark Henry ducked just in time and The Undertaker was slightly injured. In the next move, Mark Henry attacked him. The Undertaker fell and for some time, Mark Henry dominated the game. After this, he charged back and didn't give a single chance to his opponent. They moved out of the ring and The Undertaker attacked him with a series of punches and other moves. Mark Henry was simply not able to match up to The Undertaker.

It was at that moment that I entered the stadium. I was wearing a black lower along with black boots. All of a sudden, all eyes were on me. There was a hustle and bustle in the air. The backstage team, the management near the ring and everyone else looked at me with an expression of shock. Who is he? The question was visible in everyone's eyes. The Undertaker looked confused. He was absolutely clueless about where I had come from.

There was a thunderous music. All the people, including the wrestlers, the commentators and the crowd were eyeing me. I marched towards the ring. I raised my hands and roared like a lion.

As I headed towards the ring, more confusion spread in the stadium. When I entered the ring, The Undertaker was outside it. He then entered the ring and came near me.

I didn't move back even by a small fraction when he came near me. I was a bit nervous, as it was my first fight and that too, with someone like The Undertaker. For a few seconds, there was silence between us. He looked deep into my eyes, trying to scare me with his fearful looks. But it didn't affect me. After a few seconds, he suddenly punched me on my face. His punch didn't affect me at all and I continued to stand there unbothered. He was shocked to see that his punch didn't have any impact on me. He seemed confused. He hit my face again. But I didn't fall. After that, it was my turn. I hit him right in his face. Just a single punch and he fell down.

The crowd, the commentators and the management were shocked to see The Undertaker lying flat on the ground, as a result of a mere punch. When he stood up, I attacked him before he could gather himself. I dragged him towards the corner, ripped apart the turnbuckle and threw him on the steel and he fell down again. This time too, he didn't get a chance to strike back as I kept hitting him. It felt as if he was becoming numb. He lay on the ground, unable to rise. This was the time for me to acknowledge the crowd. I raised both my hands and faced the crowd. He then tried to get up. When he was about to get on his feet, I kicked him and that was it. He did not try to get up again.

I had defeated him.

I had defeated the great Undertaker!

I stood over him, with both my legs across his body and raised my arms as a sign of victory. The commentators were shocked. They said that never in their life had they seen a person who could do this to The Undertaker.

The Undertaker had been defeated by an amateur wrestler!

Defeating him made the entire world notice me. It was followed by instant appreciation from all over the world. All of a sudden, I became a superstar. My fellow wrestlers warned me that I shouldn't mess with The Undertaker as he was one of the most powerful wrestlers in the game. He was the undisputed king of the WWE. However, quite contrary to what they said, I learnt that he isn't known in the world just because of the fear he instils and the way he fights, but also for his good sportsmanship. His reaction to his defeat was completely different from what I had expected. He personally came up to me and wished me good luck for the future. I was lucky to get my WWE break with a legend like him. It was a dream start for me.

Life changed completely after my victory. All of a sudden, I was known to the entire world and people began to look at me with awe. The other wrestlers envied me. My huge physique had become a subject of interest all over the world. I was happy with the kind of appreciation I got wherever I went and when I observed myself in the mirror, I felt happiness from within. The physique which used to be a subject of mockery at one time, turned out to be a blessing for me. There was success and glory all around me. I felt at each moment that life couldn't be better. I was given a celebrity status. The entire world seemed to be proud of my achievement. The WWE was thunderstruck by my success and everyone in the organization was speaking about me. I had never felt so respected before—be it in the WWE, the media or the outside world. I was given a completely different treatment by the people. The story of my success had reached all across the US and well beyond it into the world.

I got a large number of phone calls from India. My phone would buzz throughout the day. There were calls from my near and dear ones, mediapersons and politicians to congratulate me on the success. My countrymen were happy about me and there were celebrations in the nation. The people from my district, Sirmour, felt proud of my achievement. My parents, siblings and my wife were ecstatic to see my achievement but they were also worried about my safety.

I watched as the media frenzy increased with each passing day. The Indian media broadcast the fight over and over again. Various media channels reached my village as they wanted to broadcast the views of my villagers on my success. The entire village was crowded with outside broadcasting vans and the atmosphere, I was told, was like a big village fair.

They also called me in the US. Most of the time, I answered their questions. However, there was a tragic development. It so happened that I had to urgently come back to India when my uncle passed away. This was a painful time for my family and all of us were sad because of his sudden demise. But somehow, the channels got the news that I was present there and soon, the village was filled with reporters. They wanted to talk about my success and they wanted the villagers to be happy for me. They wanted to take my interview in person, with the villagers cheering, dancing and celebrating my success in the background. How are people supposed to be happy in times of agony and pain?

This was when I felt how insensitive the media was and about the price one has to pay for such success. One channel representative even started playing a drum and told the villagers to dance around me. They were least bothered about the situation we were in. They were only interested in promoting their channels and getting high television rating points (TRPs).

I was hurt and so was my entire family.

After the rituals were over, I wanted to spend some quality time with my family. This did not seem possible in India with mediapersons chasing me wherever I went. Going abroad was the only option. So I decided it was time to stay away for some time till things settled down. I took my entire family on a tour to Europe. All the other wrestlers from the WWE were also on vacation. However, the environment wasn't different in Europe. The Great Khali, as I was now known, received an altogether different treatment there and was appreciated there as well.

I began to realize that with great success comes the responsibility of managing it.

21

The WWE Championship

After my debut on the WWE stage, I continued to fight in a large number of matches. Some of them turned out to be memorable ones while some others are better forgotten. But I kept learning from each and every game. Every victory and every loss taught me a lesson. I tried to analyse my strengths and weaknesses from every game and used them to my advantage. With every match, I learnt new moves to entertain my audience and new ways to defeat the opposition.

I also travelled all around the world. I had everything I could have wished for by then—money, respect, love and identity. I knew God had been kind to me. He had given me more than what I deserved. However, I soon realized that a human being's wishes never come to an end.

Perhaps, this is how life is—we always wish for more, struggle for more and live for more.

At that time, for me that 'more' was the World Heavyweight Championship within the WWE. For a wrestler, this is the biggest title one can achieve. The desire to be the ultimate champion grew stronger in my heart. A person who has the desire to turn his dreams into a reality is ready to tread on the toughest paths no matter how difficult it might be. I was ready to give my all into achieving this dream. Being in the WWE, I knew that I was on the correct path to take me to my ultimate goal.

For eight years, I had dreamt of being a part of the WWE and I was living that dream. I knew that I could even make the dream of being the ultimate champion a reality. In a year, due to the intensive training and continuous matches, I had become a lot more skilled and had built a formidable physique. But I kept working hard. In fact, I increased my workout hours and became more resolute in my practice. All I needed was a chance to make my dream come true and I wanted to be absolutely prepared when it came.

That chance finally came in the Battle Royal match in the year 2007. It is one of the toughest matches in WWE, wherein twenty wrestlers fight with each other in a single ring for the title. In the end, the wrestler left standing in the ring is declared the winner. I was nervous but I was also confident and had my faith in God. Also, I ensured that my nervousness didn't impact my game at all. My strategy in this game was simple as always. I just knew that I had to thrash every wrestler competing out there and win the game. I didn't care about how powerful the opponent was. I just needed to throw him out of the ring.

In that match, I had to compete with some of the strongest competitors of the WWE like Batista, Kane, Mark Henry and many others.

The match started and I did exactly what I had planned. I kept throwing the other wrestlers out of the ring. I was focused. I was confident. And I knew what I had to do.

In the end, I won the match, eliminating both Kane and Batista in a single move.

Do you want to know what the commentator said after the match? 'Presenting to you, the World Champion, The Great Khali!'

It was astounding to hear that. I could not believe my ears. I had become the champion of the champions and it was a beautiful feeling. I can't express in words how I felt at that time. This was one of the greatest moments of my life. This was the moment I had been living for and for so long. Everyone saw my moves, my power and my aggression but nobody noticed my tears—the tears of happiness as they slowly made their way through the corners of my eyes. I was so happy. I wanted to dance. I wanted to sing. I just wanted to celebrate the biggest success of my life.

And I did.

To this day, if someone asks me about the happiest moment in my life, I talk about this win as the biggest dream I could have ever lived.

22

A Visit to My Homeland—India

May 2008

Just a few months after I had won the World Heavyweight Championship, I had to visit India for some shows in New Delhi and Mumbai. India is the land of solace, a country which I can proudly call as my own. It is because of this country that I became what I am at present. The people here are so loving and caring that they leave their day-to-day activities just to watch and support their favourite sports star. The intensity and love shown by them is magnanimous and worth cherishing forever. Thus, I accepted the offer readily. I had to stay in India for a month. The tour was going to be long and with only two shows, I would get a much-awaited break.

As soon as I landed in India, I saw a sea of people at the airport. There were a large number of representatives from the media, too, and it was a pain for the security officials to securely get me out from the airport. I had to wait for more than an hour. The officials tried different ways to clear the passage, so that I could move out. But the fans were adamant. They wanted to catch a glimpse of me. Had it been possible for me at that point of time, I would have surely met each and every one. After all, they had come to the airport just to meet me.

After trying for more than an hour, they were able to get me out of the airport, but when I exited, a huge crowd stood there as well. Many of them had garlands and posters in their hands and I was overwhelmed to see so many people waiting for me. The car in which I had to leave for the hotel was hardly at a distance of 50 metres from the exit gate but there were thousands of people even within that length and as soon as I moved out, they began to cheer for me. I was excited to see their happiness. Somehow, I managed to get into the car and was taken to the hotel, where arrangements had been made for my stay.

I was happy to know that at that time, Sachin Tendulkar, the god of cricket, the master blaster, was also staying in the same hotel. Being a sportsperson myself, I always admired the way he played. When he got to know about my arrival, he came to meet me. He is the best example of humbleness. He is such a gem of a person and I was happy to meet him.

As I had come to India after a long time, there were many people who came to meet me like politicians, film directors and producers, and company officials, who wanted to sign me for their brand endorsements. My relatives and friends also came to meet me. There was a huge assembly of mediapersons waiting outside the hotel and they wanted to interview me. The hotel management told my team to leave the hotel after a couple of days. According to them, the large number of visitors and mediapersons was creating problems for their guests. We tried to make them understand that we didn't want to disturb their guests, but how could I say no to anyone who had come to meet me? However, they were firm in their decision.

Seeing this, we decided to leave the hotel and when the media asked us the reason for it, the public relations team told them the actual reason. The hotel management found themselves in trouble then. How could they deny that this had happened? They seemed to realize the blunder they had made. After this, the senior-most executive of the hotel came to my room, apologized and requested us to stay in the same hotel. He assured us that necessary arrangements would be made from their side. I was happy to stay back.

The next day, a show was scheduled to be held at the National Small Industries Corporation (NSIC) ground in New Delhi that could accommodate thousands of people. However, the crowd that finally arrived was so huge that there was a risk of a stampede. There was no space left to accommodate more people in the ground. Even in the WWE games, I hadn't seen such a huge crowd. The show was an instant success. My followers showered me with love and I was excited to be with them.

However, the same night, something unnerving happened, which frightened me and everyone in my team. After the show in New Delhi, I was to leave for Mumbai for another show. But that night, the WWE officials received a threat to cancel the show immediately. This was indeed a serious situation. There was a huge risk involved in conducting the event in Mumbai as we had already seen the size of the crowd in the earlier event. We knew that in the case of any chaos, it would be impossible to handle the situation. We couldn't risk thousands of lives. However, neither could we cancel the event. The tickets had been sold and reimbursement was not possible. After a long discussion with the WWE officials and the local police, a team of specially trained commandos were flown in from the UK. Finally, the show happened at Mumbai and it was another successful event, but a lot of caution had to be taken to ensure the safety of everyone.

It was in Mumbai that I met T.K. Rajeev Kumar, the National Award-winning director. He offered me a role in his upcoming movie. He also briefed me on the storyline. I did have an immediate interest in the story as it was supposed to be based on my life. Moreover, it was an opportunity to work with a genius like him. The offer was amazing and there wasn't any reason to refuse. However, there was just one glitch and that was the lack of time. I had to leave for the US for a month. We discussed the available dates but were not able to come to any conclusion. The next day, he called me up again and assured me that the shooting would be completed within the small time period in which I would be available in India. I couldn't be happier. I agreed immediately and we planned to begin shooting from the next week.

There wasn't much of a discussion or thought process involved before signing the movie. I have always wanted to do new and different things in life. Had I not done so ten years ago, I would have continued to be a constable in the PAP. I always like to be a part of new ventures as it's exciting to work in different domains. It gives me great pleasure when I learn new things and become a part of something different or unique. When I decided to sign the movie *Kushti*, there were a few people who told me to give it a second thought. They told me that I had done Hollywood movies in the past and doing a low-budget Indian movie would affect my reputation. But I didn't pay heed to them as I have never based my decisions on others' views.

The shooting for the movie commenced and I had a great experience with the entire unit. Though the kind of luxuries I enjoyed while I shot for Hollywood movies wasn't there, I was happy to work in a Bollywood movie. The crew members were friendly and they provided me a great environment to work in and I completed my sequences within two weeks. I was happy that the people of my country would get a chance to watch my movie in my own language. Through this movie, I got a chance to connect with the people of India. I had seen the love of my fellow countrymen at the airport, where people from different states came to meet me and since then, I wanted to do something for them. This was my small attempt towards that aim.

Everything seemed to be going on the right track at that time. I was happy that my visit to India had been amazing. After the shooting was completed, I returned to the US. I was excited to go back. In a month, I had got a chance to revisit my roots and enjoy a much-needed vacation. I felt refreshed but little did I know that on the other side of the globe, a conspiracy awaited me.

23

The Kiss Cam

2008–09

My life has been a series of mixed experiences and every instance of happiness has been preceded by misery and every success has brought with it its share of controversies. What does one expect after achieving a major victory from the people around him, be it in his personal or professional life? Love, respect, appreciation and a positive environment where one can enhance one's capabilities. Everyone in this world strives for these things. It is something which makes a person believe in himself. It is something which gives one a feeling of self-satisfaction and encourages him/her to keep working to achieve higher goals. But what if you observe that the people with whom you work, the people you visit each day and the people, who form a part of your day-to-day activities, develop jealousy towards you and show disrespect? What do you do when you find that these people spread petty controversies to hamper your success?

After winning the World Heavyweight Championship, I walked away with a large number of victories. It was one of those phases in life where my career was at its peak. My fans were always supportive of me and wherever I went, I had a huge fan following. They called me the strongest person in the world and as months passed by, my fan following leapt exponentially across all corners of the world. Whenever I went for a match along with my fellow wrestlers, the crowd would go crazy seeing me and sometimes, it got difficult for the organizers to control them. Many a time, I was told to exit through a different gate from the airports and other public places as there was always a huge crowd waiting at the entry points to catch a glimpse of me.

I started getting more offers from Hollywood, Bollywood, television, commercials and so on. At one point of time, my popularity increased to such an extent that my fellow wrestlers and some others from the organization began to get insecure. They looked at me as a threat to their career. However, I made sure that I was always dedicated to my organization, to my work and I always followed their advice as I wanted to support them to the fullest. I was also absolutely dedicated to the people who had provided me the opportunity to succeed. I was devoted to the WWE in a way similar to a devotee dedicated to his God. I never got involved in bootlicking. I was not involved in flattering my bosses. Neither did I expect this from anyone. I had lived my entire life on my own terms and I was not going to do anything that my conscience deemed wrong.

I wasn't aware that at that time a fierce storm was coming my way, a storm which could vanquish me. It was not evident initially, but I saw it later. I was caught in a loop where I was made to stay away from the fights in order to curb or control my increasing popularity. Some people in the organization had conspired against me. They wanted to ruin my reputation which I had built all through these years.

I felt that the Kiss cam did nothing but hamper my increasing popularity. The Great Khali suddenly turned into a person of comic interest. I felt that I was there not to fight but to make people smile and laugh. People started talking about me not as a wrestler, but as a 'kisser'.

This was also the time when my contract with the WWE was about to end. They wanted to renew the contract with me under some conditions, but most of their terms were unacceptable to me. They wanted me to get their prior approval before I acted in any movie or commercial. I had invited a lot of criticism from the management for acting in a Bollywood movie. I was criticized for not having taken permission before doing so. Going forward, I was not to do any movie without prior permission. Not only this, the decision to either accept or refuse the offer would rest with them. It meant that they would have the final say in all the professional decisions in my life and I had to accept them. I had lived my entire life on my own terms. In my journey from a labourer to a WWE champion, I had never been pushed to do anything by anyone other than my inner instinct. Even when I was poor, when nobody was with me and when I was an object of mockery for others, I had never allowed anyone to overpower me. But now, I had everything in life. I had millions of people behind me, who loved me with all their heart. Those people were my pride and my aim was to serve them whether it was in the US, India or any other corner of the world. I felt that, the kind of person that I was, I couldn't let any organization decide how I did that. Hence, I did not renew the contract.

They didn't accept my refusal. They wanted me to continue working for the WWE. Initially, they must have thought that I would accept their terms and conditions easily. But now the ball was in my court and I decided not to continue with them, given their reluctance to accommodate my needs. I just could not accept their attitude. For me, life was about exploring. I wanted to explore each and every bit of it, every field that I got a chance in. I felt that, my conditions for signing the contract were reasonable and I was not asking for anything extraordinary. I asked for a two-month period of leave every year to rest and look after my family and to have the complete right to work wherever I wished to during those two months. Other than this, I asked for no intervention from their end while signing contracts for films, television shows or endorsements. It would be completely my choice. There were a lot of negotiations that took place after that. Finally, after a number of discussions and meetings, I signed the contract after they agreed to my terms and conditions.

A few days after signing the contract, I was told by the management to enter into an event under the name of 'Kiss Cam'.

Kiss Cam was an event in which I had to kiss the WWE divas on a random basis. I was not interested in such activities, but I was told that being a part of the entertainment industry, we had to entertain our viewers. They tried to convince me that such a publicity stunt was a necessity and it was something which was practised rampantly in the entertainment industry. They assured me that there was nothing wrong with the event and that it was nothing more than just a harmless kiss.

Kissing random girls was something I had never even imagined doing in my entire life. I am a simple person dedicated to my wife and was at that time not interested in getting publicity like this. Plus I was uncomfortable doing this stunt. However, I was dedicated to my profession and had to trust my organization and follow their instructions. Finally, after a lot of reluctance, I accepted the offer. At that time, I didn't know the effects of my decision. But eventually, it turned out to be my biggest mistake, one that I was going to repent for my entire career.

24

When Big Show Cried

September 2009

One of the biggest demons in a human being that has the power to shatter all kinds of bonds, be it personal or professional, and create differences between people is jealousy. It is rightly called a green-eyed monster. It is an emotion which leads to hatred and affects everyone negatively.

In the game of WWE, I have always felt negativity from one end or the other. It is only natural. My beliefs are quite different. I have always believed that if someone toils really hard, God will always be with him or her to show the right path. Nobody can stop that person from being successful. As far as my profession is concerned, victory and loss are part of the game. On some days, we stand victorious and on other days, we might have to taste a bitter failure. I always took each and every loss of mine positively instead of being depressed over it and being jealous of the victors. Every loss has taught me a lesson about my weaknesses and how to master them. I actually learnt from the victors. I wish others had the same spirit but all are not the same. Some people tend to pull the other one down instead of going up themselves.

One such incident is my backstage fight with Big Show. It happened immediately after the end of a tag match which was held in Arecibo, Puerto Rico, in September 2009. There was a six-man tag team match, with three wrestlers in each team. The Undertaker, Matt Hardy and I were on one team and Big Show, Chris Jericho and CM Punk were on the other team. During the game, I hit Big Show on his chest and under the impact of my punch, he fell down. Watching this, the crowd immediately began to cheer for our team. In the match, Big Show and his team had to face a shattering defeat. Though it was just a game and winning and losing were a part of it, it turned out that Big Show didn't take the loss in the spirit of a true sportsman.

After the match, I noticed that he was looking at me differently. At that time, I didn't know what was going on in his mind. Hence, there wasn't anything to be worried about. After a while, I went back to the locker room and being a little tired, I thought of getting some rest before changing my clothes. I was sitting there on a bench when all of a sudden, he came into the room and screamed at me. Initially, I assumed he was joking. I tried to smile, hoping that he would smile back too. But he kept on shouting for a few minutes and accused me of using his exclusive moves during the game. I didn't pay any attention to him as we were well aware of his behaviour. He always dominated every wrestler. However, he became more agitated as I ignored him and he started using abusive words. This was not at all acceptable to me. I was still not fluent in English, especially with the usage of cuss words, so not knowing anything better to say, I replied by just saying, 'Same to you.'

At this, he charged at me all of sudden and tried to hit me. I dodged to save myself but before I could understand anything, he punched me with full force. Though I dodged, he managed to hit me on my face. I was shocked. I had never imagined that Big Show would be so unprofessional. I considered him as a professional wrestler and expected better of him. This was not only a physical attack on me but an assault on my self-respect as well. All of a sudden, I was wild with rage and in response, I hit him hard on his face. The blow was strong and not only did it shake him but also made him fall to the floor.

By now, I was more than angry with him and didn't want to let him go so easily. Even though I regret it now, I had been overpowered by my anger then. I leaned towards him to teach him a lesson but before I could hit him again, the other wrestlers intervened and pulled me back. I was angry and tried to break myself free from their grip but they were too many. They tried to calm me down and control the situation. Even after a minute, Big Show was still on the ground. My anger could have wreaked havoc that day.

The funny part is that after a few minutes, when I had calmed down a bit, I noticed that most of the wrestlers present there were only in their towels! Some were taking a shower and some were changing when the fight started and they hadn't even got the time to put on their clothes. Big Show got up by now. He sat on the bench and then out of the blue, started crying out loudly. This was unbelievable. He sobbed and cried like a baby, hiding his face with a towel. The people who stood around sniggered. A person as powerful and well-built like Big Show can't be expected to cry like this. We were used to seeing him boasting about his powers and dominating others but this was something that was a funny treat to the eyes.

By the evening, the news of this incident spread to every member of the team. A fight inside the locker room wasn't a normal occurrence. The news that Khali hit Big Show was on everyone's lips.

A couple of days later, I was called to the chairman's office. McMahon and the director were there along with Big Show. I was questioned about the incident. I had nothing to hide. I was truthful and knew what I had to say. I narrated the entire incident honestly. A lie can be manipulated, but truth can't be, that's my belief. A truth will remain a truth forever. I told the management that I would not take this kind of unprofessional behaviour in the future. All the while Big Show was sitting there quietly with his head held low. In the end, he was sent back with a warning.

Later, Big Show felt sorry about the incident and it was clear he was genuinely apologetic. If I wanted, I could have sued the company and Big Show for this incident. However, that was not important for me. What was most important was my self-respect and it has always been so. Therefore, I accepted his apologies and shut this chapter forever.

Years later, we did some more shows together.

25

A Reality Show

The second phase of the WWE did not turn out that well for me.

I was offered a role in the Hollywood movie, *MacGruber*. I wanted to take up this opportunity, so I tried to negotiate with the management to get a few days off. I was bound by the contract, so I could not take leave without their final consent. I was stuck.

However, I have always wanted to do different things in life and refusing the role in such a movie would have been a step backwards in my career. Ultimately, I had to take a decision. So, I decided to extend my working hours. According to my usual schedule, I had to work for the WWE four days a week, which included the fights and other events. The remaining three days were booked for my personal training. I signed the movie and utilized two out of the three days allotted for my training for the movie. It was unacceptable to me to not do what I wanted to do.

However, this schedule was tough as I didn't have time for proper rest, but I was committed to it. I worked continuously for three months without a single leave. I had to make up for my loss of personal training on other days. Finally, I successfully completed the shooting and did not compromise on any of my responsibilities towards the company.

Later in the year, I couldn't take up an offer from Colors TV channel to be a participant in *Bigg Boss* Season 3. It was one of the most famous reality shows in India and I had only heard about the programme from my friends. Though I had never seen it, my sources informed me that participants of the show had to stay in a house together for a period of ninety days. I knew that due to my contractual obligations, I wouldn't have been able to be a part of the show. Moreover, since it was an event to be held outside the country, it would have been difficult to manage.

Then again, in 2013, I missed another opportunity to act in the movie, *Escape Plan*, where I had been offered a role against Arnold Schwarzenegger and Sylvester Stallone. It was one of the biggest offers of my life but the movie demanded from me complete dedication for three to four months. This was again not possible for me.

Fortunately for me, in the year 2011, the production team of Colors India approached the management directly. They wanted me to be a part of *Bigg Boss* Season 4. The channel team negotiated with the management and made them aware about my fan following in India and the popularity of the show. They also offered a good sum of money along with a promise to further promote WWE in India. After many discussions, they came to an agreement and that was how I participated in *Bigg Boss*.

I wanted to enjoy every part of my stay in the *Bigg Boss* house. For me, it was a different kind of world where I had to do nothing. No long and painful workout sessions, no travel, no fights, no shows—all I had to do was to be in the house and chill out. For the initial few days in the house, I kept observing the other participants. I did not know them but they already knew me. Most of them were a part of one group or another in the house and gossiped all the time. They used abusive words and involved themselves in fights over silly issues. I wasn't able to understand why they, the so-called celebrities, did this. I am not the sort of person who loses his temper so easily. I, however, didn't want to do anything stupid which would hamper my image or affect my career in a negative manner. I just knew that I had to enjoy every minute of my stay without getting involved in any fights. Sometimes there were situations where I felt like I would lose myself and become a part of that nonsensical chaos. I was mocked, and I was instigated by the other participants, but I tried to keep my cool. And I emerged successful in my endeavour to remain composed. I was in the house till the very last and was declared the runner-up, and Shweta Tiwari was declared the winner.

I wouldn't say that my stay there was all that bad. It was also fun to be a part of the show. I even enjoyed the punishment given to me in the show which was to wash clothes and cook food for all the members for two weeks. Another incident which I remember and now makes me laugh was my argument with a fellow participant.

These few arguments were without malice at the end of the day; there were only naughty bantering. I'm glad though that I survived till the end and was loved by the public.

26

The Most Precious Gifts of My Life

My Wife—My Life, My Love

Harpinder has always been the person whom I have admired more than anyone else in my life. She has always supported me in all the endeavours of my life. It is tough to be the wife of a sports star as I am hardly at home. With my hectic schedule requiring me to travel to various corners of the world, there are lots of responsibilities that have to be managed by her on her own without any support from me. But she has always managed them so smoothly that I have never even had a hint of my family's day-to-day problems and challenges. I am thankful to God that I have her as my better half. Be it my personal endeavours or professional ones, she has always stood by my side and never complained about anything.

Initially, when we got married, she stayed back at my home in India while I went to the US. She stayed in Dhirana, my native village. An urban girl, who had spent all her life in a city, she had to get acquainted with the lifestyle of a small village. She couldn't understand their language and she wasn't accustomed to the village lifestyle, culture or customs. Their life was totally different. She had to do a lot of hard work as there were fewer facilities in the village and being a city girl, she had never done all this before. But she perfectly adjusted with everything around her. She never complained to me about anything and whenever I talked to her on the phone from the US, she was cheerful. She never told me that she was trying hard to cope with the difficulties back in my hometown. It was only when I came back to India and saw her pale face did I realize it. Due to the differences in lifestyle, her complexion had become dark and she looked weak and fragile. It was then that I understood how tough it must have been for her to be in a new place, a new environment and lead the kind of life which she never had before. And that is when I decided to take her to the US.

Even after we came to the US, she adjusted to the new environment quite easily. In fact, she played the role of an efficient manager in my life. At that time, I faced certain difficulties due to the language barrier, so it was my wife who managed everything for me. Be it the scheduling of events, connecting with people, attending and responding to my mails or talking to the media, she did everything with utmost care. She managed my phone calls, the schedule of my matches and the people from the WWE directly spoke to her for any matter. She even took care of the minutest details. She was a wife, a manager, a friend, a consultant and my whole world. She was my lifeline. She took the lead role in my life without any demands. Had she not been in my life, I would never have become what I am today.

During the tough times, she always stood by me, holding my hand. She supported me emotionally. There were times when I felt low, but she motivated me like a friend. The most important thing we had in our relationship was trust. We trusted each other blindly. I was always out there in the world of glamour, but Harpinder never questioned me regarding that. She never felt insecure. She knew that whatever I did in life, I would not do anything which might hurt her. We understand each other and support each other.

Avleen—My Baby

The most beautiful feeling in the life of any couple is the moment when for the very first time they hold their child in their arms. The birth of my daughter, Avleen, was one such moment for both of us. We were in the US during the time of her birth and I took leave for two days for it. The doctors had told us that Harpinder would have a caesarian delivery. They also informed us about the risks involved, as due to some complications, the operation had to be done in the seventh month of pregnancy. Though we were a little worried, even during those times, Harpinder displayed amazing strength. She not only tried to not show her worry but also assured me so that I wouldn't get tensed. She kept discussing the name which we would give to our child. We had already decided the names even before Avleen was born. Being far too excited about her birth, Harpinder and I had already made a number of plans before she was born.

After a complicated surgery, Avleen was finally born in the seventh month. When I saw her for the first time, I suddenly felt that my world was now complete, that my family was complete. She looked like an angel. Holding her for the first time gave me immense pleasure. I felt like I could hold her and gaze at her cute, little dewy eyes for an entire lifetime. She was small, so small that I was scared that she would slip out of my hands. Harpinder and I had to wait for twelve long years in order to get this happiness. Hence, Avleen's birth was all the more special for us.

For the first two hours, Avleen didn't open her eyes. Immediately after the birth of a child, the baby is expected to cry. But Avleen was silent, not for a few minutes but for more than two hours. With every passing minute, I got more and more anxious. My girl was born and that too, after so many complications, and now she lay silent. For the entire time, I kept looking at my little baby, not averting my eyes even for a split second. Finally, after an anxiety-laden two hours, she opened her small, round eyes. I was sitting just next to her. It seemed that she was looking at me. The sudden surge of happiness on seeing my child open her eyes for the first time was unexplainable. It was unlike any other feeling in the world. She was an angel, a blessing which God had sent for me. I felt blessed that God had given me an opportunity to look at my own reflection, a part of me. The feeling of being a father is out of this world. It is absolutely beautiful. I kept looking at my baby. After some time, I took out my mobile phone.

'I have become a father,' I texted all my near and dear ones.

To say that I was happy would be an understatement. On that day, I laughed more than I had ever done in my entire life. After the initial few hours, the doctors carried her to an incubator and informed us that she would have to be kept under observation for three weeks as she was a premature baby and had to be taken extreme care of.

Harpinder was released from the hospital after one week but Avleen wasn't. She had to be in the incubator for another two weeks. We were disappointed for having to go home without our daughter and my wife wasn't ready to leave the hospital without her. She wanted to stay with her, see her, look after her and take care of her. She wasn't ready to leave Avleen alone for a single moment. Even I didn't want to, but the doctors told us that the baby needed extreme care for the next few weeks and that we couldn't stay with her all the time. This scared both of us but even after the insistence of the doctors, Harpinder still wanted to stay back at the hospital. It was for the first time that I saw her act in such a stubborn, childlike manner. But her behaviour was quite expected for a woman who had become a mother after such a long time and that too, when her baby was in danger. I understood her condition but I also understood what the doctors had told us. It was again a fight for me, a fight where I had to establish the balance between the requirements for my daughter and my wife's will.

For years we were without a child and now, God had accepted this prayer of ours but our baby was on the verge of getting separated from us. Hence, I had to do what was best for Avleen. I decided to listen to the doctors. It was time for me to take on the role that Harpinder had performed for me for so many years. I had to take charge and take care of her. I had to ensure that she did not feel frustrated and could live her life normally.

Somehow, I took her back home but she felt dizzy and weak. She was gloomy the entire day, and kept asking me to take her to Avleen. She cried over and over again. I tried to console her, but to no avail. I knew that she wouldn't budge. In the evening, she started to complain that she was feeling weaker and had to go to the hospital. I understood that the anguish and turmoil in her heart affected her health. It was heart-breaking. So, I took her to the hospital where she rushed to see Avleen. I requested the nurse to remove our baby from the incubator. When she saw her, Harpinder started weeping. I then took Harpinder for a check-up; all her results were normal. She wasn't ready to leave the hospital even after that. After explaining to her and assuring her that we would come and meet Avleen every day, I finally took her back home. For the next two weeks, we went to the hospital five times a day and it was only after two weeks that we got to bring our little baby back home with us.

Since then, there was no looking back. Our little angel is the source of happiness in our lives. She is and always will be the single most precious thing that our worlds revolve around.

27

CWE Academy—From Aspirations to Reality

January 2015

In our life, there are moments when it is important to take some tough decisions. Moving out of a comfortable and settled life is difficult as one has to make a decision between letting certain things go and choosing to give wings to a new dream.

I went to the US years ago with a dream to undergo training for professional wrestling. Those were the times when I didn't have enough money as my resources were limited. I wasn't even sure at that time whether I would be able to achieve my dream as I was alone in a new country. There wasn't anyone to support me, help me or guide me. I was insecure, but passionate. Over a span of several years, after facing tremendous difficulties and with the support of my fans, I finally became The Great Khali.

However, a question always seemed to echo in my mind, why don't we have great training academies for wrestling in

India? Having a population of 1.3 billion and being a nation where so many youngsters love to watch WWE, there wasn't a single training academy for professional wrestling in India. What if somebody wants to be a professional wrestler, like me? Will he have to go through all the difficulties that I had faced at the beginning of my career? What if that person didn't have funds to go to the US for professional training? There were no answers to these questions. Dreams could die because of the dearth of resources. And now that I had seen the great heights that a person with zero resources like me had touched, I couldn't afford to let this happen! I could not see a single dream die. The problem wasn't the lack of good, passionate wrestlers, but the dearth of proper organizations to train them. For years, I had wanted to do something for my country, for my people—those who loved me, cheered for me, felt proud of me and wanted to be like me. I wanted to work for those who had dreams of becoming wrestlers. I wanted to train them, hone their skills and utilize my experience, so that they could achieve what they had dreamt and desired.

Though I had everything I could ask for in the US, I still wanted to come back to my country, live amongst my people and work for them. I had a good life in the US but somewhere I knew that if I had to provide answers to the questions that were troubling my mind for so many years, I would have to leave everything and come back to India.

For a while, I went through a lot of confusion. Leaving the US was a big decision and I needed to be strong enough to leave everything which I had built there. But ultimately, I made up my mind. This was how I came back to India to set up the CWE (Continental Wrestling Entertainment) Academy and to give light to the dreams of thousands of aspirant professional wrestlers.

I decided to set up CWE in Jalandhar, the place where I learned wrestling for the very first time. I started my hunt for the right location in Jalandhar. I finally found a large stretch of land on the outskirts of Jalandhar, near Rama Mandi.

It took about six months to set up the academy and ensure that all amenities were available. I personally supervised every detail. I wanted to see that the trainees had what they needed at the CWE. I was well aware of the interest that my people had in the game of WWE and the sport of wrestling and sure enough, as soon as the people got to know about the academy, a large number of applicants came in. I like to believe that I have created a space where aspiring wrestlers can now learn and live their dreams. And in a way, I am also living my dream with them.

Spending time in the academy with the students is fun and exhilarating, but it is also challenging. The difficult part is to ensure that every student has a trouble-free learning. Many a time, I have to personally ensure that they are having a comfortable life. Training students of different age groups—right from the age of five to thirty—is a huge task. But I know that in the past I have handled every challenge successfully and that I will continue to do so throughout my life.

I am happy with my life in India. When I enter into the ring, train kids at CWE Academy and share my experiences, I feel a great satisfaction. I feel as if my hard work has finally paid off. When I see the dreams of becoming successful wrestlers shining bright in their eyes, I feel as if my life has got a new meaning. I wish to see many champions from India fighting and winning wrestling matches all around the world. It is said that the journey of life never stops. You may end one phase of life but another might just be waiting around the corner, ready to be explored and conquered. After I quit

WWE, I felt elated as I knew that I was about to begin a new phase of life, one which would take me on a new journey—to produce hundreds and thousands of wrestlers like me in my motherland by providing them a chance to flourish and see my country shine bright on the world map.

Acknowledgements

All of us have dreams but few are actually able to achieve it. Some people are lucky to have a great support system in their lives which helps them achieve what they had set out for. My case is no different, and it is necessary for me to mention the names of the individuals without whom this book would never have taken shape.

First of all, I would like to thank my parents, who have supported me in every stage of life. Not only did they trust my convictions but also wholeheartedly supported me in every endeavour of mine. I strongly attribute qualities of hard work and honesty to them.

I would like to dedicate this book to my wife, Harpinder. I wouldn't have been what I am without her support. She continues to be a constant support system at every point in my life.

I would like to thank my close friend, Ashutosh, for not only cheering me on in life but also inducing positivity in me.

A special thanks to Mehal Singh Bhullar, who is a guru, mentor, friend and everything else to me. He has always stood by my side, even when I had nothing.

I would also like to thank my friends, Ranbir Singh and Manish, for constantly believing in me and supporting the several initiatives undertaken by me.

In addition to this, I would like to specifically thank my friend, Natalya, whose support during my WWE journey remains unparalleled. All the fun-filled moments shared with her, including the road trips, the dance parties and our gossip sessions are forever and fondly etched in my mind.

I would like to make a special mention of my co-author, Vinit K. Bansal and his entire writing team—especially Tanmay Kulshrestha, for having played a crucial role in the completion of this book.

Furthermore, I would like to thank Sanjeev Mathur and Nikita Roy, whose valuable inputs played a great role in enhancing and shaping the book.

I would like to specially thank my literary agent, Suhail Mathur from The Book Bakers, for working hard to find a suitable publisher.

In addition, I extend my thanks to Vaishali Mathur, executive editor, Penguin Random House India, and the entire team at the publishing house for their enthusiastic support.

Last but not the least, I would like to thank you, my reader and my fan, without whom my journey would never have been so fulfilling.